Book Description

What does Socialism mean to you? What about Marxism? Despite almost two centuries of complicated discussion and debate, the terms are often used as if their meanings are obvious.

For the layman, these words are wrapped in so many layers of controversy and contradiction that simply discussing them with friends and family can explode into contention and strife.

Americans, even those who consider themselves to be politically astute, can easily become overwhelmed by the sheer amount of disinformation and misdirection surrounding the current cultural discussion, and this is entirely by design.

In Unmasking American Marxism, author Casey Amnon takes readers beyond the slogans, laying out the true origins of Marxism and Socialism and how their meanings in our modern political landscape have been twisted far beyond historical meanings.

With this crucial resource in hand, readers will be able to recognize the inherent bias of today's media conglomerates and how they are complicit in knowingly disseminating false information to millions of Americans.

Unmasking American Marxism shines a spotlight on these tactics and arms you with clear, objective facts in order to make political decisions that best line up with your interests, and not let others make those decisions for you.

Regardless of your political views, background, class, race, or sex, if you want to educate and equip yourself with the tools you need to pull back the proverbial curtain, Casey Amnon wrote this book for you.

Unmasking American Marxism

*How the Powerful Subvert Ideas &
Manipulate the Masses*

Casey Amnon

Table of Contents

Order Out of Chaos

References

Introduction: Forewarned is Forearmed

Imagine, if you will, a pentagram.

If you are unfamiliar with the word, chances are you're familiar with the symbol itself. A pentagram is simply a five-pointed star, made up of continuously intersecting lines. When encased inside a circle it is called a pentacle.

What kind of things comes to mind when someone mentions a pentagram? For average Americans, it is often associated with witchcraft, Satanism, demonic activity, and evil.

Though it is not widely discussed, you can trace the roots of the pentagram back to 3000 BC, in ancient Mesopotamia. From there, this polygon would experience an incredible journey that stretches from the dawn of civilization to the modern day.

In ancient Babylon, the pentagram was a symbol of Ishtar, the Queen of Heaven and the goddess of war, love, beauty, and justice. In the Eastern Levant, the pentagram might have been used as the seal of the Kingdom of Jerusalem. Because ancient Hebrew was made up of only consonants, the city's name was written as, "ירשלם" (YRŠLM). Examples of this can be found on pottery from ancient Judea, where the five letters are stamped between the five points of a star.

The ancient Greeks used the symbol as a marker of well-being and mutual recognition. The Pythagoreans, faithful followers of the renowned Pythagoras, called it "Hugieia" which translates to "health". This stems from an ancient Greek myth wherein Hygieia, the Goddess of health, glimpsed a pentagram and recognized mathematical perfection.

In China, the pentagram is an ancient symbol representing the five "phases" or elements. It is called Wu Xing. The pentagram is used in traditional applications of Feng Shui, acupuncture, and Taoism.

Early Christians believed that the pentagram represented the five wounds of Christ. The five-pointed star was also said to protect against unclean spirits. While pagans, occultists, and other spiritual practitioners use the pentagram in various rituals, the symbol does not stand for the dark and shadowy motifs that are attributed to it.

When used by self-proclaimed Satanists, the pentagram is turned upside down, within a double circle, and often includes a goat head inside of the star. This Satanist pentagram is called the Sigil of Baphomet. Satanists of a more secular bent believe the three downward facing points represent a rejection of the Holy Trinity and religion in general.

But what does this have to do with American Marxism, you ask? If you'll kindly bear with me just a little longer, I promise this will pay off. Now, back to that pentagram.

Does the information I've just covered change how you feel about this symbol? Did it surprise you? Why or why not? You might find yourself asking another question now: How did a symbol as old, and entrenched in lore as the pentagram come to be recognized in such a narrow context?

That explanation begins back in medieval Spain, with the genesis of the infamous Catholic Inquisition. Most people know about the Spanish Inquisition, but that particular period of western history was not the first example of its kind in Catholic Europe.

The first inquisition was sanctioned by Pope Lucius III in 1184 and the second in 1231 at the behest of Pope Gregory. Two hundred and forty-seven years later, the most famous and longest-lasting of the Catholic Inquisitions began in a newly united Spain. In 1478, "the Catholic Monarchs" Isabella I and her husband Ferdinand II reestablished an inquisition during the apogee of their "Reconquista" (Reconquest) of Andalusian Spain.

The pious monarchs declared that this new inquisition would root out heresy and spread the true faith across their new nation. While the main targets of the edict were Spain's Jews, pagans were in no way excluded from judgment. This final inquisition stretched into 1807, when the Emperor Napoleon occupied a conquered Spain. The centuries-old practice would not end until 1834.

In 1854, a former Catholic Priest named Alphonse Louis Constant wrote *Dogme et Rituel de la Haute Magie* under the pen name Eliphas Levi. In this work, Alphonse made the first claim that a pentagram turned upside down was representative of evil. He asserted that the symbol attracted dark spirits and entities.

Arthur Edward Waite, who co-created the Rider-Waite Tarot Deck, translated the book into English as *Transcendental Magic* in 1855. It was then that the image of the upside-down pentagram as a symbol of evil was fully realized in the American consciousness.

Fast forward over a century, to the 1970s and '80s. American media was awash with stories of serial killers and their unfortunate victims, including the infamous Son of Sam, David Berkowitz, who claimed that a demon had possessed his neighbor's dog. He testified that the demon then convinced him to brutally murder people.

The infamous Nightstalker, Richard Ramierez, was known for leaving a pentagram "calling card" on all of his victim's bodies and he would go on to flash the words "hail satan" at the jury during his highly publicized trial.

Fascination with, and fear of, these dark and violent themes lead to an uptick in interest in all things occult, and during this period the pentagram was solidified in a misidentified state. There it remains, the victim of a centuries-long smear campaign.

Blood and Soil

For now, I want you to forget the pentagram. Instead, I want you to imagine a swastika. It is very hard to imagine a modern-day symbol that can inspire the same visceral reactions as the notorious swastika.

In the 19th century, after archeologists discovered what they believed to be the fabled city of Troy in modern-day Turkey, German translators began to notice distinct similarities between old Sanskrit texts and their own language. This birthed several theories about a common Indo-European language and ancestry. The roots of these discoveries eventually inspired the Nazi's "ubermensch" mythos.

Soon German intellectuals were dreaming up a race of prehistoric, white-skinned, blonde-haired heroes they called Aryans. Several antisemitic German factions were unsurprisingly drawn to these theories, mainly as a mechanism to legitimize their white ancestry and their prestigious Germanic genes.

Those minds responsible for building the Aryan archetype were drawn to the ancient Indian swastika as well. They claimed that the many examples of this symbol, found all around the world, served as proof of their supposed master race. No one could know then that this beloved, ancient symbol would one day symbolize some of the most heinous acts of the 20th century.

The Nazi Party of Germany chose the symbol as their own and used it in their new flag design in 1920. The First Reich replaced the former flag of the Northern German Confederation with a straight-armed, hooked cross they dubbed a "Hakenkreuz." By 1933, when the Third Reich rose to power, the Nazi flag and its swastika design were officially named as the national flag of Germany, until after Hitler's defeat.

The black swastika configured on a red field is indicative of the Nazi slogan "Blut and Boden" or "Blood and Soil". The flag symbolized the party's nationalist goals of uniting a defined racial structure (the blood) and a destined settlement area (the soil). Adolph Hitler himself took credit for the flag's design.

Though its recent history has led many to regard the symbol as a sign of evil, it is also a revered religious symbol. In ancient Hindu texts, the 'svastika' is said to represent the unconquered sun, good fortune, and the infinite possibilities of the universe.

The oldest example of this misunderstood symbol dates back 15,000 years, to what is now modern-day Ukraine. In 1908, the tusk of a long-dead mammoth was unearthed there. It had been carved into the shape of a bird and displayed a pattern of connected swastikas across its surface.

No one knows for sure what the swastika meant to those ancient Eastern Europeans, but thanks to this archeological discovery, we do know that the original swastika far predates even the earliest origins of the Nazi Party.

Early Christians used the swastika to represent Christ's victory over hell, death, and the grave. This new usage was a slight variation from the Norse religious tradition, where the swastika represented Thor's hammer.

Like with many other pagan symbols and traditions, the Catholic Church would adopt and adapt the swastika for their own purposes. In cathedrals, graveyards, and mausoleums all over Europe, you can see the impact this symbol had on medieval European society and architecture.

The monastery school that Adolf Hitler attended as a boy, Lambach Alley, boasted carved swastikas on its stone and wood facade. Perhaps it was this early exposure that led Hitler to crown it as the ultimate representation of the Nazi ideology. Hitler had long sought a symbol he could use to represent the Nazis, one that distanced it from Germany's deep Christian roots.

The Fatherland, which was known as the Holy Roman Empire for centuries, was also the birthplace of the Protestant Reformation. Because of these historical legacies, both Catholicism and Protestantism were well represented in the German population.

Hitler could not logically hope to blend his vision of a racially pure and ideologically unified Germany with that of Christ, who was himself a Jew. Instead, Hitler turned to the ancient swastika as proof of a storied Aryan lineage: a master race that superseded the Papists, the Lutherans, and the Zionists.

Though the symbol is of prehistoric origin and has different significances to many different religions and cultures around the world, the Nazi's appropriation would successfully reinvent the symbol as the infamous symbol of genocide and authoritarianism we know today.

We've now seen two examples of how symbols can evolve over time and shift away from their original meanings. Beyond the annals of humankind's history, in our shared archetypal consciousness, these images have been born anew, their faces changed and their history long-forgotten.

As a species, we too have undergone many transformations. Throughout this progression, we also transformed our means of communication and recordkeeping. Eventually, a new system of recording our thoughts, language, ideas, and stories emerged.

We now return to ancient Mesopotamia, where the Babylonians once carved pentagrams into their doorways. It was in this region, during the earliest years of civilization, that letters and written language systems were first created.

For the whole history of written language, from the Rosetta Stone to modern internet memes, the ideas and themes that writers and artists intend to convey can be lost to the tides of history, just like the ancient symbols of the prehistoric age. Speaking of misinterpretations, I have another question for you: When you hear the term Machiavellianism, what comes to mind?

Just a little precursory research turns up all sorts of results for the term Machiavellianism or Machiavellian. Wikipedia alone has six pages deemed relevant to such a search. The first page leads to an article on political realism, another to the psychological study of cold and manipulative behavior, another discussing Machiavellianism in the workplace, and even an article on Machiavellian intelligence.

The Machiavellian intelligence hypothesis is an evolutionary theory. It suggests the existence of bigger brains in humans is a direct result of social competition. In this theory, because early humans were social competitors, the homo-sapiens that came out on top were the ones best able to develop complex "Machiavellian" strategies, which helped them successfully dominate, procreate, and pass on these tools to their offspring.

The final link of Wikipedia's reference page leads to an article on Machiavellianism in politics.

Machiavellianism has been used for centuries in political theory to describe political figures and their corresponding regimes. It refers to the philosophy of Niccolò Machiavelli, a diplomat from Renaissance Era Italy who wrote a book called *The Prince* in 1513.

For his time, Machiavelli was a radical thinker. He used allegory, metaphor, and rhetoric to explain extremely complex philosophical ideas. His work would not be available to the whole continent until 1532 and it would not be published in English for some years later.

In the medieval period, it was a commonly held belief amongst political philosophers that a special relationship existed between legitimate authority and the morality of those who yielded it. This was a fairly common worldview, as far as feudal Europe was concerned.

Many of Machiavelli's contemporaries wrote treatises and "mirror-of-princes" books which served as self-help guides for Renaissance-era rulers. Most of these medieval authors insinuated that in order to be a good ruler of men, a ruler first had to exercise moral fortitude. They advised those in power that success would come only to a virtuous ruler, a benevolent monarch, an ethical Prince.

Machiavelli believed that this position wasn't rooted in reality. To the Italian philosopher, authority and power held the same weight. The ruler who gained power also had the right to command, no matter if he was morally upright or not.

He insinuated that the acquisition and cultivation of power should be the only concern of a ruler who wanted to remain a ruler. According to Machiavelli, you might argue about who had the right to the throne, but the truth remained that the strongest leader, not the most righteous, always won in the end.

Machiavelli was not claiming that evil rulers should be put in power. He wrote *The Prince* to better arm those who wished to use their power wisely and judiciously. To do that, the ruler had to learn how power was gained and how, once gained, it was to be best used.

His famous quote, which is commonly shortened to "It is better to be feared than loved if you cannot be both." reads in full: "Upon this, a question arises: whether it be better to be loved than feared or feared than loved? One should wish to be both, but, because it is difficult to unite them in one person, it is much safer to be feared than loved." (Machiavelli & Marriott, 2017)

This is a much more nuanced statement, one that focuses on the struggles a Renaissance ruler faced in balancing their morality with their feudal duties. Machiavelli's philosophy taught that a ruler who ignored reality to live up to some preconceived idea of "goodness" was only bringing about his destruction.

The diplomat was himself from the Republic of Florence. In many neighboring city-states of that time, republics rose and fell in the dust of the old Roman Empire. With the introduction of Renaissance ideas into the wealthy and influential city centers of the

Italian peninsula, new ways of thinking about politics and government sprang up and authors like Machiavelli were able to reach wider audiences after the invention of the printing press.

Then as now, outside of academic circles (and sometimes within them), *The Prince* is an extremely polarizing work. It deals with ideas that, during their time, would have been revolutionary, ideas that still resonate with modern-day philosophers and political leaders.

Unfortunately, many of the themes and ideas that Machiavelli wanted to impress upon his contemporary rulers don't translate well to modern political or philosophical discourse.

Even in the distant past, Machiavelli's work drew scorn from his critics, who saw evil and even demonic qualities in his writings. Seven years after *The Prince* was first published, the exiled English Cardinal, Reginald Pole, went so far as to suggest the book was written by Satan's hand.

On the Elizabethan stage, *The Prince* inspired the birth of the Machiavel, a type of dramatic character archetype that combines elements of comic villainy and satirical caricature.

Christopher Marlow had a particular fondness for Machiavels, including his famous characters Faustus and Barabus. His rival and contemporary, the Bard himself, based some of his best villains on the Machiavel archetype. Names like Iago, Richard of Gloucester, and Edmund give you a good idea of what Elizabethan audiences thought of that archetype, and of Machiavelli's legacy. Though the ideas he touched on in his writings might seem cruel or heartless when taken out of context, the whole of the work is, at its most extreme, a slice of political realism.

As said by one of Shakespeare's most famous evil-doers, Iago, in the play *Othello*, "But I will wear my heart upon my sleeve / For daws to peck at: I am not what I am." (Shakespeare, n.d.) The character speaks this line about the "daws", short for jackdaws and referring to foolish people, and how he refuses to allow them to see his true emotions or vulnerabilities. He revels in his own hypocrisy; Iago will deceive Othello, all while playing the role of a loyal friend.

The Machiavel schemes to convince Othello that his actions are in the main character's best interest. In actuality, Iago is secretly planning and plotting Othello's tragic downfall. Iago understands that authority and morality are not mutually exclusive. If he were to tell the truth of how much he hated and despised Othello, then the deceit would be unsuccessful and he would lose his power. The only way the notorious villain can succeed is to convince Othello, and everyone else, that the disguise he wears is his true nature.

"New Shapes of Your Own Choosing"

1984 was published over seventy-one years ago, in June of 1949. What would you say if I told you that this literary classic was written by a lifelong Socialist? Would it change how you view the book's message?

In George Orwell's most famous work, the author predicted a radical debasement of our human language and the purposeful distortion and subversion of all meaning. One of the strongest themes in Orwell's story explores how, despite all the surveillance and propaganda, in the end, it is apathy, ignorance, and self-deceit that stand as the true enemies of individual freedom.

His main character, Winston, begins his journey as a typical member of a seemingly utopian society, set thirty-five years in the future. It was not the only novel of its kind. Other books, like Brave New World by Aldous Huxley, Fahrenheit 491 by Ray Bradbury, and Anthem by Ayn Rand, created a rabid appetite for the dystopian genre. The evolution of that appetite led to a modern-day resurgence in the satirical commentary of a "perfect" future, marred by some invisible, unknowable conspiracy.

The knowledge Orwell relayed was hidden between the lines of a world locked in an infinite state of war and violence. The government, who Orwell dubbed "Big Brother" and "The Party," exerted complete and total control over its citizens as it monitored and dictated their every move.

1984 would go on to spend twenty weeks on the New York Times bestseller list and sell more than 250,000 copies in the first six months of its release. Audiences couldn't get enough of Orwell's hero, a simple man called to discover and rebuild the true history of the human race.

Winston comes to believe that the past is never truly erased, even when it is hidden from us; It remains buried deep in our hearts and minds, no matter how vehemently someone might try to turn us away from those universal truths or snuff them out. He realizes that under a dishonest system, only learning the truth and remembering the past can save us from falling victim to the machinations of the powerful. These lies are utilized by bad-faith actors and are meant to herd us, mainly by using our baser instincts against us.

Understanding where Orwell came from gives us a better grasp of the ideas he was trying to portray in his book. Even when it was first published, the British author was uncomfortable with the notion that so many people misunderstood what he was expressing in his narrative.

While *1984* was meant to function as a critique of Soviet Era communism, Orwell was himself a lifelong supporter of socialism and the British Labour Party. In modern-day America however, if you listen to conservative politicians and pundits, you'd think George Orwell was about as Socialist as trickle-down economics.

Some politicians in America are fond of citing Orwell's book when they pontificate on big government interference. They often bring up taxation, political correctness, indoctrination in schools, the welfare state, and the mainstream media as examples. Ironically, the real combatants that *1984* was trying to warn us against, ignorance and fear, seem to be their tools of choice to stir up political action amongst their constituents, viewers, and followers.

Like the Party in Orwell's book, these powerful individuals seek to control the present, which lets them control the past and, consequently, the future. They redefine words and phrases in ways that play on the instincts and paranoia of their intended audience. They rely on the subversion of words and symbols for political gain.

As a student of history, it still impresses me how deeply information can be buried by the sands of time and how far those who want power will dig to unearth them, always searching for lost artifacts and relics to redefine that will garner them more influence and control over the masses.

They hide their found treasure's true history and try to pass it off as proof of their dishonest doctrines. A tale as old as time, and a scheme that can net some great results for the proverbial scavengers.

Much like the swastika and the pentagram, these unearthed clues to our pasts must be recognized and called by their true names. If not, they can eventually be recycled, like *The Prince* and *1984*, to stoke our primal fears and desires: to trick us into frightened subservience.

If you educate yourself, instead of reacting and playing into the hands of those who want to manipulate your fear, you can make decisions without worrying about these propagandist tricks and act in accordance with your best interests.

When it comes to this particular hustle, ignorance and fear can be used as effective shields. In America, our grifters have perfected the art of brandishing them against public outcry, and their political enemies.

Chapter 1: Pointed Fingers and Loaded Guns

It can be a strange feeling when you learn something about a subject that you have previously misunderstood. The ugly truth stands in stark contrast to the simplified and oft-repeated definitions you once believed.

Much like how fables and parables of the distant past are repeated to children as a means of behavioral conditioning, the half-truths in these cultural games of "telephone" can aid in the conditioning of adult behavior as well. Instead of warning against real dangers, our words, ideas, and cultural identities are used as bait to stoke our fears and influence our everyday decisions.

In times of polarizing political discourse, this rank manipulation can stir even the most apathetic voters to decisive action. Hardly any definitions have been recrafted so effectively as the terms "Marxism" and "socialism," and, in modern times, few buzzwords can inspire the same blanket vitriol and disgust. If you ask your average American for a concrete meaning of either term, the responses would range from the uninterested to the stark raving mad.

The main reason for this rampant mislabelling is that political actors purposefully use a certain subset of words incorrectly, without much care for their actual definitions. They use these terms to mobilize your more vulnerable instincts, the ones that are triggered by fear.

Other than Marxism and socialism, various terms like communism, fascism, anarchism, Stalinism, postmodernism, and neo-Marxism are poorly understood by the masses. The interchangeable use of these terms, to serve as rhetorical and propagandist tools for dishonest politicians, pundits, and commentators has ensured that the majority of Americans don't understand the truth behind their definitions or their histories.

Unfortunately, this absurd and shallow understanding of political theories and the Western bastardization of certain socio-economic analyses has transformed them into mere buzzwords and sound bites. They are dishonestly defined to meet the ideological requirements of various propagandists.

But if you dig deeper into the tumultuous politics of humanity's past, if you study the facts for yourself, no longer do these oft-misinterpreted theorems seem so frightening or dangerous.

Once you realize the motives of those who seek to rewrite our history, it's almost impossible not to notice how entrenched we are as a nation in mistruths, half-truths, and outright lies.

To understand those motives, however, you'll need to find out what they are. Though the faces and eras change, the goals of those in power rarely do. If you recognize this, you can see how those in power have always been in a secret battle for our hearts and minds, since before Machiavelli put his radical philosophies down on parchment.

The Locomotives of History

Karl Marx was born on May 5th, 1818 in the city of Trier. At the time, Trier had a population of about 15,000 and was the oldest city in all of what is now known as Germany. Back then, Trier was a part of the Kingdom of Prussia.

Until its dissolution in 1918, Prussia was the premiere state of the mighty German Empire. It was also the dominant force responsible for unifying Germany in 1871. The storied origins of Trier, and its contemporary history, no doubt helped to foster Marx's lifelong dedication to the study of history.

During the Napoleonic wars, Trier was occupied and annexed by France. Because of this occupation, the principles and ideals of the French Revolution would take root in Marx's childhood home. Naturally, this meant Trier was much different than most other German cities.

Once its citizens were given a taste of constitutional liberty and freedom of speech they were loath to return to the totalitarian rule of the German Empire. When Napoleon was defeated at Waterloo, Trier (and much of the Rhineland) was incorporated into Prussia, despite their misgivings.

When Marx was a child, the once-wealthy region was experiencing a period of tribulation. Though the rest of Europe was in the midst of the Industrial Revolution, Trier had very little industry to speak of, and when its once prosperous vineyards went, so did the city. High unemployment rates led to an upsurge in crime, prostitution, homelessness, and emigration.

Knowing this, it's not surprising that a young man like Marx might get caught up in the utopian, socialist doctrines of Revolutionary France, doctrines that found a receptive audience in Trier.

In 1835, when Marx was seventeen years old, he began his secondary studies at the University of Bonn. The university housed seven hundred students and acted as the intellectual hub of the Rhineland region. The romantic principles of the Enlightenment were alive and well at Bonn, and an eager Karl dove right in.

Much like the fraternity members of today's educational institutions, Marx joined an organization of young men who called themselves the Trier Tavern Club, which was essentially just a group of drinking buddies. His zealous participation in this group once landed him in the University "Prison" for twenty-four hours, on charges of "disturbing the peace of the night with drunken noise" (McLellan, 2006)

Even before his first year at Bonn was finished, Marx's father decided that his son would now transfer to the University of Berlin, no doubt because of the trouble Karl had brewed up during his first year away. Assured that this would set his wayward son on the right path, Heinrich patiently waited for the end of the semester. Marx eventually returned to Trier in the summer of 1836. During that time, he was engaged to Jenny Von Westphalen.

Though Jenny was four years his senior and her family was of much higher social status, the two of them bucked social norms and traditions by insisting on getting married anyway. Jenny's father would still take a little convincing, however. Baron Von Westphalen would not acquiesce until 1837. Marx again left Trier in October of 1836 to begin his studies in Berlin.

The capital city was much different than Bonn and Trier, the two places that had thus far shaped young Marx. It was here that he would meet philosopher Frederich Engels, though not for almost six more years.

According to Engels, the Berlin of that time "with its scarcely formed bourgeoisie, its loud-mouthed petty bourgeoisie, so unenterprising and fawning, it's still completely unorganized workers, its masses of bureaucrats and hangers-on of nobility and court" had an ever-changing cultural and social hierarchy (McLellan, 2006).

His search for gainful employment would lead him to the field of journalism. In 1842 Marx began work as a journalist for the radical newspaper Rheinische Zeitung (Rhineland News). The paper was often censored by the government for its revolutionary ideologies. It was this job that allowed Marx to first outline his early views and ideas on socialism.

Marx would go on to marry Jenny in 1843. The newlyweds were soon forced to flee Prussia after Karl's newspaper was banned by the Prussian government. The paper had published an article criticizing the Romanov dynasty of neighboring Russia and was subsequently shut down. This was not an unfamiliar scenario in authoritarian Prussia.

Karl and Jenny moved to Paris, France where Marx became co-editor of the Deutsch-Französische Jahrbücher (German-French Annals). After its demise, Marx would go on to work for yet another radical newspaper called *Vorwärts!* (Forward!). *Vorwärts!* had ties to the League of the Just, which was an underground collective of artisans, philosophers, and workers.

Looking back at his upbringing and the nature of his contemporary world, the works of Karl Marx and the political ideologies they spawned seem like almost inescapable conclusions. Even someone like me, who has been reading Marx's work since college, was amazed at the many parallels I could draw between the life of Karl Marx and my own. I was equally fascinated by the unique, yet relatable circumstances that led him down his path to American infamy.

It still fascinates me how much modern-day Americans seem to vilify the progenitor of Marxism, almost as much as they vilify the doctrine itself. We are taught from a young age to praise and admire the forerunners of our American government as heroes of democracy. These men spoke truth to power and freed us from the chains of colonial England. Yet, like Marx, their true histories are rarely discussed.

These were landowning, wealthy men of high social standing. The majority of working-class Americans have more in common with Karl Marx than they do with George Washington or Thomas Jefferson. This statement is not meant as an attack on the founding fathers of America; They studied and drew from several of the same humanist thinkers that inspired Marx and many of his contemporaries.

This does not change the fact that Marx's ideologies, initially forged in the fiery furnace of the Industrial Revolution, come from an author whose story more directly mirrors the lives of everyday Americans, then and now.

After the tragic death of his father, Marx was forced to make his own way in the world. He married a woman, and together they shared seven children and thirty-nine years of marriage. They struggled together and dealt with obstacles both great and small.

All the while, Marx never lost sight of a dream that had been forming inside him since he was but a strapping lad. That envisioned solution to the age-old problem of socio-economic inequality would eventually come to fruition.

For good or ill, it would be realized and immortalized in Marx's writing. It would go on to influence and inspire millions of people to question the truth of their reality: a reality, Marx imagined, that had reigned supreme since the birth of civilization. For every person inspired by Marx's doctrine, however, there were many still who feared and scorned it.

Criticism of Marxism, Marx's works, and Karl Marx himself, is in no way a new pastime. In his own time, and over the last 138 years, there has been no shortage of critics standing in opposition to the ideas presented in Marx's various works.

The irony of this is that many of the people who deride his ideologies in our modern age have never really been introduced to them. If they have, they don't tend to reference them using the context in which they were initially intended.

"From Delusion to Destruction"

Funnily enough, when researching sources for this book, I came across one with a similar title, from the Foundation for Economic Education. For reference, the FEE is a Libertarian-leaning organization that was founded by Leonard Read in 1946. It holds the unique distinction of being the oldest free-market think tank in the United States.

The book in question is titled *"Marxism Unmasked: From Delusion to Destruction"*. It is a collection of lectures by Doctor Ludwig Von Mises, delivered at the San Francisco Public Library in the summer of 1952.

Ludwig Von Mises was an Austrian historian, economist, and sociologist who was born in 1881, two years before Marx's death. Von Mises was a proponent of Classical Liberalism, a forerunner to the modern political ideology of Liberalism.

Von Mises is widely known for his studies focusing on Praxeology: the analysis of human choice and action. In 1940, Ludwig emigrated from his Austrian birthplace to a new home in the United States. It was here that he lived until he died in New York at the age of ninety-two.

When he was thirty-eight, Von Mises presented his writings on "Economic Calculation in the Socialist Commonwealth." From this paper came the beginnings of his eventual book, entitled *Socialism: An Economic and Sociological Analysis*, published in 1922.

By the mid-1950s, various Libertarian political movements in the west began to draw inspiration from Von Mises' various works. These works were very influential and are considered widely responsible for the readoption of Classical Liberalism as a political philosophy in post-war America.

This period would come to be known as the Cold War era, referring to the sustained international tension between the Soviet Union and the United States following the conclusion of the Second World War. The combatants of this Cold War included the United States and its respective allies, who were referred to as the Western Bloc, along with the Soviet Union and their allies. They were likewise known as the Eastern Bloc. The Cold War began shortly after the end of WWII, and wouldn't end until 1991, with the fall of the Soviet Union.

It is called the Cold War because there were no physical battles directly waged between the two budding superpowers throughout this entire 44-year period. However, they did engage in some regional conflicts, known as proxy wars, wherein they provided aid and funds to foreign nations in conflict, as a means of weakening their respective rival.

These proxy wars were the direct result of widespread fears and anxieties over the possible nuclear holocaust that might erupt if the United States and the Soviet Union were to engage in conventional methods of warfare. They were effectively loopholes, ones that the former allies brazenly used to allow for a no-holds-barred, geopolitical smackdown the likes of which the world had never seen.

In America, the legacy of a progressive political shift had rapidly changed the face of mass media in our country, most notably the new medium of television programs. Ease of access to information began to drastically impact the public's opinion of their government and contributed to a combination of rising skepticism and war-weariness among the American people.

To circumvent this cultural shift, the United States government resorted to the practice of granting large caches of weapons to insurgent forces that were hostile towards their Soviet rivals, like they did in the Soviet-Afghan War. Meanwhile, the Kremlin soon discovered that it was cheaper to align themselves with foreign nations and political factions who were antagonistic towards the United States, much cheaper than combatting NATO's influence through direct military intervention.

The two most infamous examples of this proxy warfare are the Korean War and the Vietnam War. Otherwise, both superpowers engaged in more indirect acts of aggression, such as trade embargoes, psychological warfare, espionage, and complex propaganda campaigns.

This rivalry even bled into recreational pastimes, like the Olympics and other sporting events. Their competition to see who would make it to the moon first drove the United States to win the historic Space Race. That metaphorical race was much less foreboding than its blood-soaked cousin, the Nuclear Arms Race, at least at the outset.

To thinkers like Von Mises, the political future of the world looked like a very disturbing place. Western liberals and conservatives feared the "Red Menace" of socialism, which seemed to be lying in wait behind every shadow, ready to swallow the world into its collectivist maw.

In all fairness, they did have tangible reasons to believe such things, given the contemporary political climate of the time. After World War II, all of Eastern Europe came under Soviet influence in one way or another. By the end of the 1940s, China was being governed by Chairman Mao Zedong and his People's Republic.

The year that Von Mises gave his lectures in San Francisco, American forces were fighting under the UN's banner along the 38th parallel, between the warring factions of North and South Korea.

The United States, alongside their South Korean allies, was trapped in a tragic stalemate with the North Koreans and their Communist Chinese allies. In Indochina, the French were still embroiled in a seemingly infinite conflict against the forces of Ho Chi Minh and his guerrilla army of Communist soldiers. Further west, there was a sharp rise in the number of intellectuals that now believed the study of history pointed towards socialism as the cure for modern society's many hardships.

Establishment-minded scholars watched in horror as the membership of Communist parties rose all around the globe, leading to a phenomenon that history would come to call the Second Red Scare. Governments in both the New and Old worlds were turning increasingly to policies of intervention and social welfare in their quest to eliminate their societal ills. Without a doubt, Marx's teachings were one of the main catalysts behind this rise in the adoption of radical, political philosophy as a means to achieving true equality.

These "radicalized" philosophers believed in Marx's ideas regarding certain universal truths and their fated role in the prophesied demise of capitalism. They believed Marx's truths, his laws of humanity's social and historical development, would aid in the triumph of socialist ideals and pave the way for his vision of a Communist utopia. This would first have to be prefaced by a revolutionary dictatorship of the proletariat.

To Marx, the term 'proletariat' referred to the working class in general. It gained its name from early 19th-century philosophers, who first recognized similarities between the modern working class and the proletarii of antiquity. These original proletarians were a social class within the hierarchical structure of ancient Rome. It comprised freeborn Roman citizens who owned very little or no property.

It was a liberal, Swiss historian and economist, named Jean Charles Léonard de Sismondi, who initially applied the term to describing the plight of the modern-day working class under capitalism. Marx cited Sismondi's writing on the subject numerous times in his works.

According to Marx, the dictatorship of the proletariat would act as the shield between the goals of socialism and the machinations of the deposed ruling classes. It would serve to prevent the capitalists from regaining their power.

Led by an imagined vanguard of the most politically advanced and class-conscious proletarians, the working class would garner and exercise political power against their natural enemy, the bourgeois.

The vanguard was also, theoretically, responsible for the reeducation of their fellow "proles." Moreover, the vanguard had a duty to help elevate them to higher levels of consciousness and critical thought, to better break the chains of their former bourgeois mentalities.

Bourgeois was derived from the Old French word *burgeis*, which translates to "walled city". In Old French, a similar term, *bergeis,* means "town dweller". That word was derived from the Old French *bourg*, meaning "market town". *Bourg* was originally modified from the Old Frankish word *burg*, which translates simply to "town".

You can find many similar variants of this word and its meanings in several different European language groups, including in Polish, German, English, Dutch, and Spanish.

For our purposes, the bourgeois are defined as a social class who are historically at odds with the proletariat. The term is comparative to the idea of the middle class, or upper-middle class.

Traditionally the bourgeois have always lived comfortably, distinguished from the working class by their higher levels of political, cultural, social, and financial means or "capital."

The bourgeois are sometimes divided into three groupings of upper, middle, and petty-bourgeois. The idea of a "middle-class" of any kind is directly intertwined with the history of cities and their role in the rise of mankind's highly-developed civilizations.

Marx believed that the sweeping social changes brought on by the Industrial Revolution had provided the perfect opportunity for the bourgeois to take control of the means of production and ensure their future supremacy over the proletariat, their hegemony.

In the 1950s, while many people openly rejected the policies of socialist and Communist governments, they still subscribed to the principles of socialism as a means of making the world a better place.

Venerable minds of the Cold War period, like Von Mises, were haunted by the thought of educated Europeans and Americans coming around to the idea that capitalism, if left unchecked, would lead to social injustice, exploitation of the middle class, wealth inequality, and widespread misery.

As he hailed from Austria, Von Mises saw firsthand the toll that Soviet socialism took on Eastern Europe and Russia. He was opposed to the overarching premise of socialism from very early on in his career.

Mises believed that socialism's early critics were on the right path in their condemnation of comprehensive economic, social, and government planning. The commonly held belief amongst this subset of philosophers, authors, and political figures was that such planning would only lead to the bitter sting of tyranny and subjugation.

They believed that the idea of "The State" controlling all aspects of employment, production, and distribution, under whichever social class maintained supremacy, would lead to monopolistic corruption. That corruption would inevitably leave every man, woman, and child on Earth at the mercy of political authority.

These critics also believed that socialist ideas about "abolishing" freedom of enterprise and private property would snuff out the self-interested motives that drove the spirit of innovation and industry in the free market.

Mises did not believe that socialism as a political theory was workable in practical application. He doubted that the central planners of socialism, like Marx's Vanguard, would ever be able to rationally and successfully govern the complicated affairs of social and economic life.

He proposed that only a market economy, where production is spurred on by supply and demand, could drive businesses and entrepreneurs to effectively organize and make use of their available resources, while also letting them maintain freedom and autonomy.

Mises believed that a free market, by design, would regulate itself to rationality through supply and demand. In his eyes, under a system of central planning, such inherent checks and balances simply could not exist. This is because the prices of free markets are established by the buying and selling preferences of all market participants.

Buying and selling are only possible, according to Mises, with the existence of private ownership. Under these premises, the voluntary exchange of currency, goods, and services was entirely at the discretion of the respective owners, not any governing body.

Throughout my time researching this book, I have read many critiques of Marx and his ideologies, the historical events they inspired, and the impact they've had on society. Out of all these critiques, I can truly say I enjoyed Mises' the most. His work on the subject is poignant, insightful, and well researched.

He formulates all of his arguments in the wider scope of collectivism versus individualism and impresses on his audience his belief in the singular importance of individual sovereignty to provide a better future for society. Mises was adamant in his stance that to surrender one's liberty and property to an all-powerful state only courted certain doom.

Throughout the series, Mises stays staunchly loyal to the values and ideals of Classical Liberalism, ideals he believed were the true means of achieving global prosperity and well-being for all.

His approach in presenting these lectures differs greatly from the bulk of the modern examples I use as source material for *Unmasking American Marxism*. It presented more rational, well-researched positions against socialism, Marxism, and communism and argued against their legitimate definitions. Even if you disagree with Mises' findings, it's hard to deny that his opinions are backed by thorough research and a valuable understanding of the material being discussed.

Much to my surprise, the further back I investigated into the history of Marxism's critics, the more sense those critics began to make. In 1896, another Austrian economist named Eugen von Böhm-Bawerk published *Karl Marx and the Close of His System*. In the book, Böhm-Bawerk investigates Marx's analysis of value and concludes that Marx's law of value inherently contradicts itself.

He denounces Marx's willful downplaying of supply and demand's role in determining market prices. Böhm-Bawerk claimed that the majority of his work was too ambiguous to use in practical political applications. He asserted this ambiguity was deliberate on Marx's part.

Böhm-Bawerk's book is well crafted, if not a bit more difficult to get through than Mises' collection of lectures. It is considered to be the leading example of a classical critique of Marx's book *Das Kapital*.

The majority of critiques that came after the publication of *Karl Marx and the Close of His System* followed in the Austrian author's footsteps. Böhm-Bawerk even served as a professor to Ludwig Von Mises at the University of Vienna.

There can be little doubt that his teachings left a lasting impression on young Mises, one that would follow him across the world, to the San Francisco Public Library, where he would carry on his former professor's tradition of delivering scathing critiques on Marx's principles and theorems. A history teacher who was granted a scholarship to attend the lectures wrote to *The Freeman* magazine in the fall of 1952.

> The lectures themselves I found provocative, stimulating and highly rewarding...I am not trying to say that I became converted completely to the set of ideas that Dr. Mises and the Freeman represent. But I do say that any student or teacher of the social sciences who fails to think deeply on these ideas is negligent and ill-informed, if not worse. This feeling the seminar did leave me with. Certainly, I personally appreciate some of these ideas far more than I did a month ago (Foundation for Economic Equality, 2017).

Mises' aim was not to forcibly convince his audience of the absolute certainty of his opinions, but instead to make them think for themselves. The Austrian critically examined Marx's work and vehemently disagreed with it.

Had Mises been ignorant of the ideologies he was arguing against, I would not have found myself half as fascinated, nor half as open to hearing his opinions. Because his arguments were concise, well written, and grounded in reality, I found myself compelled to finish them. Compared to some of the more ridiculous examples of critiques on Marxism that I've encountered, this one didn't read as mudslinging or a smear campaign. His concern is real, and whether I agree with any of his opinions is immaterial.

While the list of credible, academic rebuffs of socialism and Marxism, like *Marxism Unmasked,* is a long one, our next critique on Marxism doesn't come from another political theorist or doctor of philosophy.

Instead, we'll take a closer look at a contemporary of Karl Marx, the world-famous novelist Charles Dickens.

Bent and Broken Into a Better Shape

Like Marx, Dickens came from a middle-class family, not wealthy enough to be considered rich but not so unfortunate as the poorer denizens of early 19th century London. He was born in 1812, six years before Marx's birth in Trier.

Charles Dickens' childhood home was a metropolis of gigantic proportions, the shining capital of the mighty British Empire. It was arguably the center of the most prestigious capitalist nation in the world, at that time. Beneath that shiny veneer, there existed a darker, seedier side to Victorian London.

Modern inventions and technological advances were exhibited side-by-side with the archaic and brutal traditions of feudal England, like floggings, hangings, and mass executions. For those Londoners that fell upon hard times, there was no recourse to feed and maintain their families, save for turning to the generosity of their relatives or private charities.

Thousands of unfortunate souls, who had come to the city searching for livelihoods, found themselves crammed into tiny, dirty, unsafe housing projects known as slums. Raw sewage from some of these slums flowed straight down into the River Thames

Dickens' father, a clerk who often found himself unable to provide for his wife and children, was eventually imprisoned in the Marshalsea Debtors' Prison because he owed a baker named James Kerr a little over £40.

While Charles' mother and siblings accompanied their father into Marshalsea, the young boy was sent out on his own to fend for himself. He got a job at a factory in London where he labeled bottles of boot polish.

Very quickly, his boyhood had gone from one of comfortable means to a nightmare of epic proportions. Those of us in the modern world could only describe it as Dickensian. But back then, Charles had yet to pen such classics as *Oliver Twist*, *Great Expectations*, and *A Christmas Carol*.

No, back in 1824, Dickens was merely a twelve-year-old boy, forced to face the bone-chilling deprivations of Victorian London without even his family for comfort. His days and nights would have been filled with hard work and he would have had no time or money to further his education. Instead, the young boy was left to wonder if he would have enough for a roof over his head or a hot meal to eat before crawling into bed.

The idea of such a grim existence for a child is terrible to imagine, but it presented young Charles an opportunity to truly understand the steep levels of wealth inequality that plagued London. Even at that tender age, Dickens came to understand the cruel realities of the society he lived in, and those months living in extreme poverty would forever shape his work as an author.

John Dickens was soon saved by the death of his mother, who left him an inheritance that he used to pay off the most outstanding of his debts. He was then released and his son Charles was returned to his family once again. Dickens was able to return to school and leave those months of drudgery behind him.

This too reads like a scene from one of his later works, where the erstwhile young hero is saved from his plight by a turn of fate.

I used to spend endless hours in my childhood, legs dangling over my mother's recliner, reading the tales of these pitiable people, and the unexpected windfalls were always my favorite part of a Charles Dickens novel. Literary critics might claim that his plot twists are too contrived or that they are too improbable to ring true, but I can only imagine the sheer relief and thankfulness Charles must have felt to finally walk out of that workhouse and leave the abysmal conditions of the London slums.

Though he was extremely reticent to speak on those dark times in his childhood, Dickens would go on to become one of the most widely read authors in modern history in large part due to his gripping and oftentimes stomach-turning depictions of Industrial-Age London.

Charles Dickens, like Karl Marx, was a first-hand witness to the growing pains of capitalist systems in an industrialized Europe. Both men observed the rampant inequality between the upper and lower classes of their respective regions.

While Marx would shape and mold this knowledge into his philosophies and political theories, it was Dickens' works that first touched the hearts and minds of the everyman. They called to account the appalling conditions subjected upon the poor of 19th century England and those intense depictions resonated with members of the working class all over the world.

Marx himself admired the great Victorian novelists of his time, most notably the Brontë sisters, Charles Dickens, and William Makepeace Thakeray. He believed they, not the moralists or the politicians or the publicists, were the true touchstones of those universal principles that governed the evolution of the human condition.

Karl Marx shared the city of London with Dickens for twenty years, during his exile from mainland Europe, but Dickens never charted his course down the path of a political radical. He was a social reformer, in favor of changing and reshaping the existing political and social structures to address the wrongs and injustices tackled in his novels.

The author loathed social reforms that strove to punish or discipline the most impoverished of London citizens. For Dickens, reforming laws and precedents did not mean making welfare less accessible or making the conditions of the workhouses as unpleasant as humanly possible.

These free-market ideas sought to convince the masses that the bottom rung of the western social hierarchy was somehow to blame for their destitution. If they starved, they did not work hard enough or they did not deserve even the most basic human decencies.

As with many reformers, Dickens strove not to revolt against the status quo, but to convince his readers that the way forward was through compassion for, and common purpose with, their fellow man. This is never more true than in Dickens' depiction of Ebenezer Scrooge in *A Christmas Carol.*

The character begins the novel as a cruel and greedy man who cares nothing for his family, lover, friends, or colleagues. He scorns his fellow man and has alienated himself from everything that makes him human. Through his personal history, he is pushed to remember that common humanity within himself and cast off the years of trauma that have shaped him into a nearly unrecognizable monster. By the end, he is a generous benefactor of the poor with a whole new lease on life.

This redemption story is, in and of itself, an indictment of the notion that members of the upper class are devoid of the same essential qualities that define their less fortunate counterparts. To Dickens, crushing the bourgeoisie through revolution was not the option of a rational thinker. Instead, he sought to inform the public, and in doing so, enable them to speak their truth to power.

While his methods were also considered radical, he was in no way affiliated with any Communist organizations. Like many great minds before and after him, Dickens' reformist ideals sought to find a way to break free from the excesses of unrestrained capitalism, without abolishing existing power structures.

Out of these reformist traditions, new ideologies like social democracy, utopian socialism, and economism sprung up; novel avenues of political theory began to expand and take a new shape all over the western world.

For the bourgeois, this branching out of socialist thought must have seemed frightening. As capitalism likewise took shape within the scope of medieval feudalism, the ruling classes of that era did not have to look far for a historical example of one system overthrowing another.

With this example ever before them, the rich and powerful members of western society now had a common enemy to fight against. Even from the beginning, the whole affair was rather lopsided, given the massive difference in capital that existed between the bourgeois and the proletariat. These unfair advantages would help one side arm itself, while the other was busy trying to shore up its earliest foundations.

The Labor Wars Begin

It was just a handful of hours past sundown, on a warm spring night in Chicago, and the whole world had gone mad.

The day prior, the city bore witness to bloodshed and violence at a protest attended by disgruntled workers from the McCormick Reaper Works. The factory was responsible for manufacturing the McCormick Reaper, an agricultural machine used by farmers worldwide to harvest their crops.

Cyrus McCormick invented the first mechanical reaper in 1831 and his work would inevitably revolutionize the agricultural industry in the United States and beyond. By the end of the American Civil War, Cyrus was a rich man, whose company had seen a tremendous amount of success. When he died in 1884, McCormick left his progeny a manufacturing empire that had grown far beyond his wildest dreams.

Despite this success, by 1886 the organization was paying its working population a pitiable salary of only nine dollars per week. Considering the workweeks of average Chicagoans were long, grueling, and dangerous, it seems exceedingly unfair that companies like McCormick refused to pay their employees a livable wage.

On average, most American workers would spend sixty hours a week at their jobs, with only one day off per week, and workers in factories like McCormick often had to deal with extremely dangerous conditions. If they were injured on the job, there was nothing to save them from poverty and destitution, even though their employers were not required by law to provide them safe working environments.

During this time, metropolitan centers like Chicago were hotspots for collectivist action. In reaction to these demonstrations, employers adopted harsh anti-union policies like hiring strikebreakers, firing and blacklisting protestors, and employing violent thugs to act as their private security guards.

They deployed spies and double agents among the workers, to betray their plans and to help spread division from within. The employers were supported in their anti-labor initiatives by politicians, municipal government officials, police departments, politicians, and the major mainstream media outlet of the time, local newspapers.

On May 3rd, 1886, workers gathered at the Reaper Works in an attempt to peacefully protest the company's practices and fight for their rights. They were supported by city union leaders and the strike itself was a part of a nationally organized campaign to demand a nationwide, eight-hour workday.

During that protest, the Chicago police stepped in to intimidate strikers and protestors. They also aided strikebreakers and "security guards" who were not above using physical violence to deal with the crowds. During the skirmish, police killed a protester and several more were severely injured.

That did not dissuade the protestors; they acted quickly to organize another protest the next day. They sought not only to bring attention to their struggle for workers' rights but to showcase the inhuman levels of police brutality the working class was subjected to at the hands of their enemies.

This time, local anarchist leaders were the most active in organizing the protest and spreading the word, one that would be held in Haymarket Square. They called for like-minded workers to join them and advised them to arm themselves against their opponents.

Over the course of the actual gathering, there was no real trouble. The Mayor of Chicago, Carter Harrison, himself attended and declared that it truly was a peaceful protest. But when the Mayor and the majority of the protestors left, a group of police officers arrived and ordered the remaining crowd to disperse. When they did not, violence broke out. Amid this scuffle, an unidentified individual within the crowd of protestors launched a bomb at the police officers.

The volley was returned with random sprays of gunfire. By the end of the ordeal, seven police officers were dead and sixty were gravely injured. It is estimated that eight civilians were killed and over thirty more were left injured. The bomber was never positively identified.

This bloodbath stoked a nationwide wave of anti-immigrant sentiment and paranoia about the motives of the labor movement's leaders. Eight prominent anarchists were arrested in the wake of the bombing. They were convicted of aiding and abetting the attacker.

Though their alleged crimes were never actually proven, and many of the accused weren't even present for the protests, four of the so-called "Chicago Eight" were hanged in November of the next year. A fifth man committed suicide before he could be executed.

Seven years later, in 1893, an attorney named Clarence Darrow petitioned the Governor of Illinois to grant clemency to the three remaining men. Governor John Altgeld proclaimed that none of the Chicago Eight had received a fair trial. He issued each of the men a pardon, though the verdict was widely criticized by Chicago's conservative press and disgruntled industrialists.

That same year, the Haymarket Martyrs Monument was built in a Forest Park cemetery, to commemorate the victims slain during the protests. These deaths did not serve to weaken the workers' resolve, in fact, they only strengthened it. Those lost in the struggle were held up as martyrs, noble souls willing to sacrifice their lives in exchange for basic rights and dignities denied to all.

In the face of these losses, the labor movement only further organized their resources, determined not to let anything stand in the way of their purpose. They continued to unite a disparate population of native and foreign-born workers from all walks of life.

People from different cultures, religions, political ideologies, and social classes stood hand in hand against the reprehensible actions of their powerful opponents. These were regular, working-class people, determined to stand up to the corruption and greed that controlled every aspect of their lives.

The cries for an eight-hour workday only grew louder after the Haymarket Affair, and by 1888 the American Federation of Labor announced they would launch a renewed campaign demanding a shorter workday. They designated May 1st of 1890 as a day of national protest and called upon workers to once again go on strike.

In 1889, Samuel Gompers, the president of the AFL, wrote a letter to the first congress of the Second International, who were attending a summit in Paris. This summit was a gathering of the world's leading socialist leadership. Gompers' letter illustrated the

AFL's plans to fight for the eight-hour workday and urged those at the summit to stand with American workers in solidarity.

They did just that, declaring May 1st as a day of international demonstration, one where workers everywhere could all unite in their shared struggles, despite their geographical distance. The Second International made this decision, in part, because of their desire to honor the memory of the fallen workers who died at Haymarket Square. Perhaps it was also this memory that helped to make the first International Workers Day such a rousing success.

In Europe, as well as North, Central, and South America, workers everywhere refused to cross picket lines and instead stood together, joining their voices to fight back against the wealthy, powerful people who sought to silence them. Though horrific, the deaths of the Haymarket Square massacre served to arouse the social consciousness of thousands and breathed new life into the international labor movement.

These newly awakened workers, the lifeblood of the global proletariat, were quickly initiated and exposed to all manner of radical ideas and philosophies. The early labor movement was chock full of anti-establishment leaders of all shapes and sizes. Socialists, anarchists, communists, Marxists, and everyone in between wanted to use this rising tide of public discontent as a catalyst for revolutionary action among the working classes.

Far from helpless, the western bourgeois fought back against this cultural shift, adopting anti-labor policies and scrambling to sully the image of their political enemies in any way possible.

One of the most effective ways of achieving that end was propaganda. Decades before the onset of the Cold War, the capitalist powers of the United States and western Europe began their offensive against the dreaded menaces of socialism and communism. Though most of us are familiar with western wartime propaganda from the 1940s or later, it might surprise you to learn how widespread the campaign of anti-Communist and anti-socialist propaganda truly was, even before the outbreak of World War I.

In 1909, the British Conservative Party, widely referred to as the Tories, published a poster entitled "Socialism: Throttling the Country." This propaganda piece showed the party's predictions of what socialism would mean for early 20th century Britain.

The poster has a solid, orange background. Upon it stands a regal-looking woman, dressed in an ancient Grecian gown. On her head rests a helmet, reminiscent of Athena, the goddess of wisdom and war. Around her waist, she wears a blue sash that reads "prosperity" in white lettering.

In one hand, she holds a silver trident; the other is flung out in distress. At her feet lies a fallen shield, with the Union Jack painted upon it. The goddess has dropped her shield because she is being viciously strangled by a monster.

The creature is depicted as standing on her shield. It is covered from head to foot with thick, brown fur. Though it stands on two legs, its face is batlike. It has severely pointed ears, a stubby tail, and long, sharp nails on the ends of its hairy toes.

After this poster was published, most anti-communist or anti-socialist propaganda began following a familiar pattern of depicting leftists as terrifying or inhuman. In pre-revolutionary Russia, communism was likened to one of the Four Horsemen of the Apocalypse. In Germany and Scandinavia, the fear of the notorious Bolsheviks inspired government agencies to depict them in gigantic proportions, with their feet straddling cities, countries, continents, and even the planet.

Unashamed at the prospect of using the same tactics as their rival bourgeoisie, some leftist leaders of the early labor movement fought back with propaganda of their own, while other labor leaders refused to do so. The roots of this ideological schism stretch back to Chicago in 1905, and the formation of the Industrial Workers of the World.

That year marked the nineteenth year since the Haymarket Affair. For many of their members, the American Federation of Labor no longer satisfied the aims and desires of its diverse population. Though socialism was utilized by early leaders to fuel the rise of the AFL, and the involvement of the Second International helped to spread their cause worldwide, by the early years of the 20th century, the AFL was vocally anti-Socialist.

The AFL had recently joined forces with the Democratic party of the United States, thereby creating alliances with their politicians on local, state, and national levels. The AFL's leadership now believed that it was capitalism, not socialism, which would provide the best path to achieving labor's goals and demands. They billed their organization as the rational alternative to collectivist-inspired radicalism.

Because so many people in the early Labor movement identified with various leftist policies, this stance (and the general adoption of Liberal political philosophy) drove many members to abandon the AFL.

In June of 1905, two hundred trade unionists, anarchists, and socialists from across the country gathered in Chicago to denounce the American Federation of Labor. It was at this convention that they founded the IWW as a revolutionary organization, dedicated to promoting worker solidarity and the overthrow of the industrialists at any cost. They chose the phrase "An injury to one is an injury to all" for their motto. This is still the organization's motto today, 116 years later. The IWW wanted to outline their distinct differences from the AFL and similar national trade unions. Where the AFL's slogan was

"A fair day's wage for a fair day's work," they encouraged their members to scrawl the words "Abolition of the wage system!" on their banners and signs. (Foner, 1986)

The preamble to the IWW's constitution states:

> It is the historic mission of the working class to do away with capitalism. The army of production must be organized, not only for everyday struggle with capitalists, but also to carry on production when capitalism shall have been overthrown. By organizing industrially we are forming the structure of the new society within the shell of the old. (Industrial Workers of the World, 1905)

The ensuing years after the IWW was founded would see the organization facing extreme persecution. Its members were targeted, deported, unjustly accused of trumped-up charges, beaten, harassed, and even killed.

These practices only escalated as the years passed, but their leadership did not balk at these systemic attacks. Instead, they pressed on, wholly convinced of their cause's merit and worthiness.

In the lead-up to World War I, the IWW ratified a motion denouncing the conflict. They printed and distributed anti-war stickers and propaganda posters to stop the United States from getting involved in the massive fray. Opposition to World War I was not uncommon in the United States, and certainly wasn't confined to the political left. Women's suffrage groups, religious pacifists, and even industrialists like Henry Ford made it well known that they wanted no part in the geopolitical conflict.

President Woodrow Wilson himself campaigned in 1916 on the merits that "He Kept Us Out Of War". But by 1917, he was busy trying to convince these various groups that, to truly bring about world peace, they would have to engage in the war to end all wars.

Once his vision was fully realized, Wilson helped to create The Committee on Public Information, a government agency crafted to favorably influence public opinion on America's entry into the war effort. This agency amounted to a propaganda arm for the U.S. government. It was eventually framed by the Wilson administration as the best alternative to the wholesale censorship of wartime news.

When Congress issued a declaration of war in the spring of 1917, the IWW was forced to curtail their anti-war efforts, and rehabilitate their public image to avoid the damage that the legislature's wartime powers could cause them.

Despite these late-stage efforts, their worst fears were soon realized. Almost as soon as Congress made the declaration in Washington, the U.S. government was already beginning its assault on the IWW. With the passage of the Espionage Act of 1917, an influx of IWW members were arrested and charged under the tenants of this new law.

The act was intended to prohibit any interference with U.S. military operations and recruitment during times of war. It also made it illegal to support the country's enemies or to support insubordination within the military.

Under the parameters of this act, the Justice Department and their newly beefed-up Bureau of Investigation raided dozens of IWW headquarters across the United States. They confiscated material from all of them, their biggest haul coming from IWW's general office in Chicago, where they picked up five tons of publications, minute books, mailing lists, and even personal correspondences.

After these raids, the evidence the Justice Department seized would prove damning enough within the context of the new law, that one hundred and sixty-six of the organization's leaders were arrested and indicted by a Federal Grand Jury on charges of conspiring to hinder the draft.

They were also accused of intimidating parties in connection with labor disputes and of encouraging desertion. Of these, one hundred and one would go to trial, appearing as co-defendants, in 1918. They stood before Judge Kenesaw Mountain Landis and every single defendant was convicted of their crimes. Fifteen of them were sentenced to prison terms of twenty years.

In May of that year, Congress passed an amendment to the Espionage Act called the Sedition Act. It enabled expanded limitations on free speech provisions during times of war. While the Sedition Act was eventually deemed an overreach of federal powers and was repealed only two years later, many parts of the original Espionage Act remain intact within the federal law code today.

Despite the multifaceted assault carried out by the U.S. government, the IWW did not disband or disappear. It would go on to reach its peak membership levels in the early years of the 1920s.

While the organization still operates in the present day, that thorough culling of the IWW's leadership in 1917 and the destruction of virtually all its records essentially wiped out the trade union's chances of achieving its original socio-political aims.

Even a reformist president like Wilson had no room for the radical idealism that the IWW represented and viewed it as a threat to the very fabric of American democracy. To fight this imagined scourge of leftist thought, the federal government employed unconstitutional means and un-democratic legislation to persecute their political enemies. This would not end with the closing of World War I.

Although the IWW was denied a chance to further influence the early labor movement, the U.S. government learned some valuable lessons during this period. Federal officials and elected representatives would revisit these means of political control over and over, using them to neutralize a bevy of other perceived threats, at many different points in our country's history.

Looking back through the lens of Marx's class struggle theories, the bourgeois appear to have effectively nullified the revolutionary aims of these early proletariat coalitions. The ruling classes had wielded their counter-revolutionary resources with devastating accuracy.

Even now, our government can use some of these same legislative caveats and loopholes to exercise Orwellian levels of political power and government surveillance. The Obama administration utilized the Espionage Act to convict several government employees on charges of leaking national security secrets, one of them being Edward Snowden, a CIA subcontractor who leaked classified information regarding government surveillance programs from the National Security Agency in 2013.

Though the Obama administration utilized the Espionage Act to investigate more than double the amount of all the previous administrations combined, Barack Obama's successor, Donald Trump, would go on to break that record during his four-year term in office.

In 2017 the Justice Department reviewed one hundred and twenty leak investigation referrals, seventy-one more than any year since 2005. In 2018 that number dropped to eighty-eight, and then seventy-one in 2019. There were at least fifty referrals in the first three quarters of 2020.

While the struggles of early American labor movements would eventually lead to many crucial protections, the tools to crush their aims and ideologies would never die once manifested. The movements were persecuted by the full might of the American government under the premise of its adjacency to leftist political philosophy.

Though workers' rights, like the forty-hour workweek and the eight-hour workday, are ones many Americans take for granted today, the early proponents of these ideas sacrificed their livelihoods, their freedom, and even their lives for us to escape the hellish conditions they were subjected to.

Capitalizing on the public's fear of socialism, communism, and Marxism, the ruling classes were able to stave off the efforts of these early labor leaders, while avoiding the appearance of violence against the working class protests they were trying to crush.

Using the Great War as justification, they wielded the American justice system as their weapon of choice in subverting the demands of workers everywhere. The fact that these same strategies are still used by the American government indicates a disturbing reality. These same tactics, used to dominate the early labor movement, are still being used by the wealthy and powerful.

It also begs the question: what fundamental rights might tomorrow's working class one day take for granted that we are currently being denied?

Chapter 2: Borrowed Fears

At this point in the book, several patterns might have begun to emerge for you.

Though today's socio-economic situation may seem novel, when you look back, it becomes apparent that human history truly is cyclical by nature. No matter the era of civilization, as a species we have come to master many skills, but none so much as repeating our failures over and over again.

For millennia, the question of why human history seems to follow the same predictable patterns has fascinated philosophers, artists, theologists, and intellectuals alike. Before written language was invented in ancient Mesopotamia, humans were huddling inside subterranean caves to look back at the stories of their past. Even in these early ages of our species, we were discovering an undeniable truth: while many things change, some never do.

This penchant for reminiscing on our pasts is an integral part of what makes us human. Unlike wild animals, humans have taken great care to ensure that records of our histories were kept, and passed down to future generations.

We converted our shared perspectives into symbols, images, and oral traditions: the sum of our collective knowledge, the wisdom and cultural heritage of our ancestors. Then we converted them further into written records. From there we used this new medium to further solidify our budding civilizations.

Because these early civilizations relied heavily on centralized governments and hierarchical social structures to function, the ruling classes of early societies were the only subset of people that held the resources and spare time to learn how to read and write. As time wore on, the upper classes began to monopolize the use of literacy to their advantage.

When studying the course of history, no matter what region of the world you choose, it becomes apparent that the consequences of this monopolization affected several different civilizations.

The lower classes of the ancient world, inherently trapped by the positions of their birth, could spare little time from their daily toils to learn how to read and write. These skills soon became a commodity, birthing a new industry in the form of scribes and clerks.

The majority of these specialized artisans were employed by the ruling classes and the position itself was one of affluence and esteem. Younger children of ancient noble and royal houses would often be educated as court scribes and would in turn use those skills to further their family's dynastic ambitions.

Once reading and writing were commodified, the demand for clerks and scribes drove up the price of the services they provided to rates that the lower classes could never hope to afford.

Though these early civilizations did not function under capitalist governments, traders and merchants were still able to carve out early financial markets of their own right under the noses of Lords, Princes, and Kings.

In most ancient hierarchies, the seat of ultimate power was held by a monarch, though just below him existed the nobility, made up of the ruler's most rich and powerful subjects. Religious and military classes came next, though many ancient religions exerted massive levels of power that rivaled even the most powerful ruling dynasties.

Sometimes, a ruler might combine the royal and religious classes and claim to rule under the authority of one or more deities. In other cases, they would rely on the warrior classes as a brutal and effective means to justify their supreme authority. Oftentimes these ancient leaders used both.

Below these ruling classes were free citizens of that particular city-state, some who owned property and some who did not. Even though they were legally free to earn their way in the world, there was very little upward mobility in ancient times, as the strict hierarchical class system was dogmatically defended by those at the top.

At the very bottom of this fiercely enforced hierarchy were the most pitiable members of ancient society: the slaves. These human beings were bought and sold like livestock, and their quality of life was determined solely by the moral character of their masters. Slaves had no rights to speak of.

The huge supply of slaves needed to sustain the ancient flesh trade was usually procured by a city-state's military forces. After their enemies were dispatched on the battlefield, conquering soldiers would then capture and enslave both defeated warriors and innocent civilians.

Like literacy, slavery soon became a commodity, one mainly utilized by the ruling classes. Slaves could be purchased for an endless variety of reasons, whatever reasons the rich and powerful could dream up.

Manual labor was often carried out by slaves, as it was cheaper to buy a slave for a one-time sum rather than to pay a free citizen the rates that their experience afforded. Purchasing domestic slaves was also much more cost-effective than hiring several servants to oversee the day-to-day management of an estate.

Though many slave owners looked after their slaves, it was more akin to someone taking good care of a car they spent a lot of money on or someone ensuring their property is well taken care of. Even so, some members of the ruling classes could afford to treat their investments as cruelly or negligently as they pleased. If they needed to purchase new slaves to replenish those lost, they could always find more. The wealthier a person was, the more savagely they could afford to behave towards their slaves, who were considered by law to be their property.

Slaves could be used as wet nurses and governesses, they could be trained as security guards to protect their owners. Some male slaves were subjected to castration so that they could guard female family members without the risk of potential rape, consensual sexual intercourse, or the pregnancies either scenario might produce.

Over the centuries, the boundaries and names of those ancient city-states grew and changed. Some would burn bright and gutter out quickly, some of their flames would burn steadily for thousands of years.

Dynasties would rise and fall. War, cultural shifts, and new religious factions would emerge to help shape the course of humanity's history, but the overarching societal structures remained the same, even as we sailed across oceans and discovered new worlds.

The power and resources accumulated by these early ruling classes would forever shape what it meant to rule, and that heritage would echo down through countless generations, surviving in various forms and iterations even into the modern day.

Since I was very young, I always found the study of history to be a fascinating thing. There was a reason I could spend countless hours exploring the familiar, yet alien, worlds of Charles Dickens novels.

For me, historical study satiated my voracious appetites for romance, adventure, and excitement, more than most of the books, movies, and tv shows I gorged on with reckless abandon.

I tried time and again, without much success, to convince my schoolmates that the lists of names and dates in our social studies books barely scratched the surface of the mysterious puzzle that was history. Once you uncovered all the missing pieces our schooling didn't provide, that's when the real fun of solving the puzzle began.

Even the brightest of my peers seemed confused as to how such things could fascinate me so much. I was by no means an unpopular kid, but I soon found that espousing my love of history made me an easy target for bullies.

It was lame to study history, it was boring and only the weird kids spent hours pouring over biographies and period retrospectives. Obsessing over Harry Potter was one thing, faithfully charting the life and times of Queen Elizabeth I was a whole different animal.

Though I eventually learned to keep my love of historical study to myself, once I started taking part in more advanced historical classes, I found a whole new outlet for my scholarly passion.

Thanks to the efforts of some truly dedicated teachers, I watched in awe as the same kids who had once laughed at my love of studying history began to discover for themselves the joys of piecing together those metaphorical puzzles.

Though they came from vastly different backgrounds, these teachers were all unified in one ideology. Along with every new puzzle piece we uncovered, they implored us to think critically about the information we were learning.

They asked us not only to digest the information we researched but to investigate our sources and contemplate their motives in analyzing said information. One particular lesson stands out from my junior year when my AP World History teacher tackled conspiracy theories and their ties to real-life historical events. We worked in pairs, each choosing from a long list of topics provided by the teacher. Many of them dealt with subjects we were familiar with, like the assassination of JFK and the urban legend that NASA faked the moon landing. But many of them we didn't recognize, even the students like me, who had spent years studying history for leisure.

My partner and I chose to cover the prohibition of marijuana. I vividly remember how surreal it began to feel, the more I delved into pot's hidden history. While I was learning about William Randolph Hurst's deliberate and dishonest smear campaign against the hemp industry in one class, I was simultaneously learning about the "terrible dangers" of smoking marijuana in another.

I was quickly able to recognize the elements of my public school curriculum that still coincided with the half-truths and outright lies propagated by Hearst and other affluent power players of that time.

I had learned enough by then, thanks again to my many talented instructors, about the history of the American educational system to know that these regurgitated factoids were labeled as curriculum standards for a reason.

From then on, I adopted a stance of mistrust in the U.S. government, one that alarmed my conservative family to no end. Growing up, I bore witness to the record-breaking rise of Conservative-run media through the lens of my mother's favored cable news network.

As a baby boomer, my mother grew up in the era of Walter Kronkite, where journalists were trusted, and the American people had faith in the facts those journalists were reporting. All my life, I remember her watching both local and national news affiliates every morning before work and every night after she got home.

Seeing as my mother was the daughter of a World War II veteran, the wife of a Vietnam War veteran, and a lifelong member of the Republican party, she prided herself on her patriotism and constantly exposed that the United States was the greatest country in the world.

As the 1990s drew to a close, my mom found herself ever more dissatisfied with network news coverage, especially where it concerned American politics. After Bill Clinton's impeachment scandal and the hanging chad saga of the 2000 election, she quit network news coverage cold turkey, save for the occasional episode of Meet the Press or The Mclaughlin Group. She soon began watching the Fox News Network. Very soon after that, it became a mainstay in our home.

I spent my formative years filtering the majority of my political opinions through the lens of a singular news outlet, with only the occasional dissenting voice of a Democrat pundit as an opposing reference point. It wouldn't occur to me until years later how unnatural a situation that was. In hindsight, like many of the numerous historical puzzles I've solved over the years, the reasoning behind my mother's blind faith in the cable news network seems painfully obvious.

Much like how the invention of the internet irrevocably changed the youth culture of my generation, the rise of television as a news medium would forever alter perception in my mother's young world.

Having grown up amidst the political tensions and pitfalls of the Cold War, my mother's generation lived in constant fear of the next atomic attack, as the United States and the Soviet Union waged their geopolitical game of chess.

As the Cold War waged on, and Americans continued to flourish under our capitalist economic system, the government held up their rivals, the Soviet Union, as an example of the communist hellscape that awaited our people if we allowed socialism even an inch of ground against democracy and freedom.

The older I got, the more I studied for myself, the more openly I began to question and denounce the unethical reporting found on Fox News. I purposefully brought up politics at family functions and beyond, baiting my relatives into useless intellectual debates.

Though she instilled in me the importance of my many civic duties and outlined what responsibilities I had to our Constitution, she also tried to pass down to me the same blind faith in our country's government that was expected of her.

As a teen, every chance I got, I flouted my defiance of the latter lesson, openly scorning the United States and sharing with her every jarring secret I could find that contradicted her worldview. With age comes time to contemplate the passions of our youth. At present, my mother and I still follow radically different political ideologies. Though mine have often changed as I matured, hers have never wavered. Even so, I have all but lost my former bloodlust when it comes to discussing politics with people I disagree with.

Knowing what I do now about the world that my mother grew up in, it's easier to understand why she thinks the way she does, easier not to get so angry and see her as an opponent to overcome. If I use the same methods that once helped me "see the light" in terms of historical study and think critically about all the relevant variables and scenarios in play, the full picture of my mother's Modus Operandi begins to emerge.

You see, critical thinking is one of the most versatile tools that we as humans possess. Uniting observational skills, the ability to use context clues, and our intuitions, critical thought has helped to solve even the most complex of humanity's many woes. Unlike the ancient world, where the flow of information was entirely controlled by the ruling classes, the modern world is awash in resources, just waiting to be explored. To some, this stands as an obvious indictment of willful ignorance in our society.

To me, it speaks more to the legacy of those ancient ruling classes, and how they were able to use critical thinking to create systems of control, systems that still affect the working class today. How is it that so many millions of people have suffered poverty, deprivation, and suffering for millennia, while the same small group of rich and powerful have exerted their vision of reality upon the masses? Like the borders of those long-lost city-states, the names and faces of the elite might change from epoch to epoch, but their motives and their methods retain an eerily similar form. They reappear again and again, to ensure the continued subjugation of the poor and powerless beneath their feet.

There is no neat, singular answer to this polarizing question, just as there is no one answer as to why humans seem to repeat the same patterns of behavior throughout every era of our history.

If you think about it critically, wouldn't it make more sense to blame humankind's cyclical habits on the social and political structures in which we are raised, instead of blaming each other, or even ourselves?

Seeing as these structures were created by the ruling classes, and are still upheld by them today, it begs another question you must ask if you're viewing the subject with a critical eye. Were these systems of control designed by the mighty, to ensure that the meek never escaped an endless cycle of mistakes and missteps?

Fall of the New Colossus

The Statue of Liberty began its life as a noble idea.

In 1865, a French poet and political activist named Édouard de Laboulaye dreamed of presenting the gift of a monument from the people of France to their American counterparts.

Laboulaye was a vocal supporter of our country and he wanted to send the statue as a token of celebration, in honor of the Declaration of Independence's 100th birthday. The poet wanted to commemorate the close relationship between the two countries and their shared love of freedom and liberty for every citizen. The Union's recent victory in the American Civil war also inspired Laboulaye to encapsulate the ideas he believed America represented.

A French sculptor named Frédéric-Auguste Bartholdi heard about Laboulaye's vision and was himself inspired to start conceptualizing the specifications for the new monument. The statue he would go on to create was named "Liberty Enlightening the World."

In 1902, a poem by Emma Lazarus was engraved on a bronze plaque on Ellis Island, her words forever crystallizing what the statue represented to millions of people around the world. Thanks to Lazarus' work, which helped raise money to fund the statue's foundation, Lady Liberty was able to beg the world for its tired, poor, huddled masses. For better or worse, the world obliged her.

Once the Great War ended, America experienced its largest influx of European immigrants to date. The majority of these new American citizens were laborers and tradesmen, but all of them had hopes of finding new lives once they passed under Lady Liberty's famous torch.

America represented a new start, an escape from war-ravaged Europe. It was supposed to be a country where everyone was free and could determine the course of their destinies. And so, the "American Dream" was born. Between 1900 and 1920, the number of factory workers in the United States jumped from 4.7 million to 9 million. This new influx of able bodies soon boosted our economy and began to line the pockets of industrialists.

Though Americans were proud of the country's ever-growing prosperity, to some the Industrial Age seemed like the end of the world. They watched as their traditions and customs began shifting and changing, their origins fading into obscurity.

Americans of that era distrusted the drastic changes taking place in the fields of science, technology, sociology, and political theory. They wanted to retain the values that made them American, that made the United States the greatest country in the world. Although anyone could become a citizen, if they weren't of Anglo-Saxon descent or didn't practice Protestantism, they were considered undesirable.

Anglo-Saxonism was a new concept, one that arose among Protestant missionaries in the late 19th century. These evangelists believed it was their God-given duty to convert the world to Christian fundamentalism; fundamentalism that went hand in hand with contemporary values of America's ruling classes.

The overwhelming majority of the day's political, intellectual, cultural, and religious leaders were from Protestant, Northern European backgrounds. Because of this, they promoted cultural and societal standards for the masses which reflected their values and protected their interests.

By 1919, the main interest of the American ruling class was avoiding a violent revolution. Two years earlier, the news of a successful revolution in Tsarist Russia had served to shock and frighten the global powers-that-be. It would serve to launch the revolutionaries responsible to new heights of geopolitical power.

While President Woodrow Wilson was busy performing his mad scramble to get the United States into World War I, across the Atlantic the Romanov Dynasty was soon to come crashing down. America had yet to throw our full might into the fray, meanwhile, the Russians (like most of Europe) had already endured years of bloodshed and loss. Though he was unpopular, and almost lost his throne in the failed revolution of 1905, Tsar Nicholas II decided it would be a good idea to take full control of Russia's Imperial forces, and personally lead them to victory on the eastern front.

He was unsuccessful and only continued to lose battles to the Central Allies going forward. Mother Russia's economy, and her citizens' quality of life, suffered when one of the Allies, the Ottoman Empire, enforced a naval blockade of the Mediterranean Sea. This blockade made it increasingly more difficult to get provisions for Russian civilians, let alone their massive armies of hungry soldiers. While the Tsar was off playing toy soldiers, his wife was busy ruling a country in crisis.

Unfortunately, Tsarina Alexandra was a German princess by birth, and so the Russian people soon came to suspect her of acting as a double agent, employed by her wicked cousin, Kaiser Wilhelm. Alexandra relied heavily on the spiritual counsel of a Siberian peasant, a mystic, the self-proclaimed holy man, Grigori Rasputin, or "The Mad Monk".

Rasputin was the only person who could grant Alexandra's son, the Tsarevich Alexei, relief from his hemophilia. Rasputin soon became indispensable, the real power behind the throne. The Russian nobility, fearing his influence would bring about the family's final downfall, arranged for his assassination. In December of 1916, Prince Felix Yussapov murdered the Mad Monk while the latter was visiting his St. Petersburg residence.

Despite their violent efforts, Rasputin's murder did not accomplish the aims of the Russian aristocracy. Nor did it save the Tsar and his family from their tragic end. The effort proved too little, too late. His death did nothing to stem the rampant corruption that plagued the Russian government, nor did it instill any faith in the Russian populace that Nicholas could improve the quality of their lives.

Though many factions of Russian political radicals had long called for an end to Tsarist rule, for the first time they were joined in their condemnations by political moderates and regular, Russian citizens. This unexpected convergence only garnered more and more strength as the days and weeks passed and eventually the mounting tensions in Mother Russia boiled over.

On March 8th, 1917 (or February 24th, according to the Julian calendar) St. Petersburg played host to a strike of textile workers. Their cries for bread echoed the sentiments of many Russian peasants throughout the land who were starving and desperate to feed their families.

They called for an end to food shortages, for an end to the Great War, and an end to the reign of the Russian Tsars. Soon workers from all over the city joined in, and within hours the streets were filled with thousands upon thousands of protestors.

The Tsar ordered the military to fire on the mobs of common people, but that didn't deter them. Soon the soldiers were refusing to follow their orders. They laid down their weapons and joined the cause, standing side by side with the marching masses. A little over a week later, and Nicholas had abdicated on behalf of himself and his son Alexei. The defeated Tsar's brother, Grand Duke Micheal, refused to take his place, and with that decision came the inglorious end of the storied Romanov dynasty.

Once the Tsarist government was out of the way, a provisional government was established, led up by members of the Russian Duma, their version of a parliament. This temporary regime immediately began to adopt liberal programs that focused on social reforms.

While they were successful in passing legislation concerning the rights of unions to organize, freedom of speech, religion, and assembly, they were not of a radical disposition. They had no intention of ceasing the war effort either, considering Russia's involvement in the Great War to be a matter of necessity. They were unable to solve the food supply deficits around the country and the entire nation was quickly devolving into chaos and anarchy. Winter passed to spring, and spring to autumn, but still, the problems which sparked the Revolution persisted. Soon the Russian people were calling for the overthrow of the provisional government, the same way they had for Tsar Nicholas.

A Marxist faction, the Bolsheviks, seized this opportunity and organized a coup after occupying the city and declaring Vladimir Lenin as their new leader. The political theorist turned revolutionary folk-hero worked to quickly end the fighting and nationalize Russian land in the name of the people. But the course of these events did not run smoothly for Lenin's Bolsheviks.

They would have to fight a years-long civil war to wrest full control of the Russian government from their opponents, but by 1923 the Bolsheviks had emerged victorious, under a new moniker: the Communist Party of Russia.

Looking back at these historical events, it is easy to imagine how the Russian Revolution, and the radical methods of the victorious Bolsheviks, could act as a powerful catalyst in creating and shaping America's foreign and domestic policies.

Though the Wilson administration and the intelligence community had unjustly persecuted the IWW, that was just one of their many coordinated offensives against leftist political factions in the United States.

The onset of the early labor movement had already alerted American authorities to the upsurge of leftist influence and philosophy among working-class citizens, and they soon began to anticipate the movements strategies and organizational methods of these diverse factions.

Where the Wilson administration had seen to the passage of the Espionage Act and the Sedition Act to better investigate and prosecute leftist leaders in the labor movement, they used another legislation, the Immigration Act of 1918, to better enable government agencies in deporting "undesirable" aliens from the United States. Anarchists were specifically targeted by the Immigration Act, along with socialists, communists, labor organizers, and other political activists.

The laws mentioned above, along with Wilson's Committee on Public Information, were proudly and ably wielded as weapons by the U.S. government, to snuff out any traces of far-left influence on the American working classes. They were not completely successful in these efforts, despite the extensive amount of collateral damage their decisive campaign produced.

In January of 1919, one of the consequences of their failure reared its ugly head, manifesting in the Seattle General Strike. What started as a protest over low wages by

35,000 local shipyard workers, soon ballooned into a unified demonstration of the city's diverse and populous working class.

Much like the Reaper Works employees over thirty years prior, the workers protesting at the Seattle waterfront would go on to inspire their fellow citizens by the thousands until their numbers swelled to 60,000.

More than a hundred local unions gathered to lend their support and their resources, headed up by the Seattle Central Labor Council. On the morning of February 6th, these determined protestors took to the streets of Seattle, effectively paralyzing the city's normal functions. Businesses, schools, restaurants, grocery stores, and more were shut down while the city's local government officials hunkered down amidst the eerie silence of the frozen city.

Union members designated as The General Strike Committee worked diligently to keep the peace and ensure that Seattle citizens were provided with food, supplies, and essential services during the strike. Those who didn't participate feared the worst. They stocked up on provisions and weapons, hiding inside their homes and awaiting the chaos and bloodshed that would surely come. The local press imagined socialists, communists, and Bolsheviks behind every corner.

Mayor Ole Hanson, who believed it was the anarchists at work behind this coordinated sabotage, called for Seattle residents to remember their American values, to turn away from foreign influence and radical ideologies. Hanson threatened to replace the striking workers with local police, and federal forces, but nothing ever came of these threats.

At the time, the national press referred to the general strike as "a revolutionary movement aimed at [the] existing government" and "a Marxian effort". The Chicago Tribune went so far as to say "It is only a middling step from [St. Petersburg] to Seattle." (Murray, 1980)

By February 8th, several unions were back to work, as their leadership feared the tide of public opinion was turning against them. Hanson's threats, and the fear of resources running out, led to many of the united strikers giving up their vigil. Many Seattle citizens were sick of the lockdowns and curfews. They were desperate to get back to their regular lives.

On February 10th, the General Strike Committee voted to end the strike the next day. The original strikers, however, those 35,000 workers who first inspired the sweeping, underdog effort, continued without faltering. Mayor Hansen was glad to take full credit for the collapse of the General Strike. The press hailed him as a hero and a patriot. While he would inevitably resign a few months later, Hansen would enjoy a successful cross country speaking tour, where he gave lectures on the dangers of Bolshevism in the United States.

While the General Strike was unsuccessful in its main aims, it served as an example of a nonviolent avenue for collectivist action. No matter that the rumors of anarchy and mass violence had been circulated by the ruling classes, the united workers of Seattle proved cool-headed and didn't resort to savagery in their quest for worker's rights.

Conversely, its inability to net real-world results was beginning to unsettle the more radical leftist elements of America's working classes. Garnering sympathy from the bourgeois through strikes had proved wholly ineffectual.

The press seemed to stand at the ready, waiting to muddy the waters with their accusations of sedition, treason, and espionage. Because of the policy decisions made under President Wilson, these accusations were like loaded guns and could bring the full force of the U.S. government down on the heads of those accused.

This was the plight of countless Seattle citizens in the days and weeks following the strike. Police and vigilantes were busy scouring the city for "Reds", an overarching label that referred to a large swath of the leftist political spectrum.

Shortly after the Seattle General Strike was announced, the U.S Senate Committee on the Judiciary commissioned a new mandate to one of their subcommittees. It was headed up by a Democratic Senator from North Carolina named Lee Slater Overman.

The Overton Hearings

Overton's committee was first put in charge of investigating cases of German subversion and sedition during World War I. When the Seattle General Strike was announced, it began studying the influence of Russian radicals in the United States, and their efforts to spread their political ideologies. The Senate wanted to know what factions were actively plotting the overthrow of the United States government.

The Overton Committee held hearings on Bolshevik propaganda for a little less than a month. Their findings ignited a flurry of fear and trepidation in the psyches of the American public. They declared that Bolshevism was an imminent threat to American values and the sovereignty of the United States government.

They insinuated that Germany, though defeated, had effectively weaponized an ideology that transformed Russia into a socialist state to bring about the destruction of America. Bolshevism's Marxist roots were evidence enough for the subcommittee to announce that the faction's aims were simply branches of German socialism, and proof of its dangerous influence on European politics.

The consensus of the subcommittee pointed to the ability of Bolshevism to unite several diverse cultures and socio-economic groups, even feuding anarchists and communists. Reformers and progressives, opposed as they were to revolutionary action, were inspired to join these movements as well, bringing large swaths of moderate Americans into the increasingly radical fold.

They prefaced these findings with eyewitness testimony regarding the Russian Revolution. They spelled out, in no uncertain terms, what the consequences of such a political movement would be. They warned of the absolution of public property and vital industries, the State-sanctioned implementation of atheism, the shackling of our "free press" and a targeted assault on the Central Banking System.

These findings were pounced upon by the American press, who were more than willing to fan the flames of fear and bigotry against any and every form of leftist doctrine they could find.

These mass media depictions were singularly effective in swaying the opinions of the American public and the veracity of their claims was soon "proven" when a string of domestic terrorist attacks rocked our nation.

Anarchist Bombings and the Palmer Raids

The spring of 1919 saw the delivery of over thirty bombs to various members of American high society by a group of domestic terrorists. A field agent of the Bureau of Investigation received one, as did John D. Rockefeller and even the Attorney General of the United States.

These bombings were organized and enacted by followers of Luigi Galleani, an Italian-American anarchist who called for the working class to use violence in their quest to free themselves. He saw it as a means to an end.

These Galleanists wanted to coordinate the delivery of the bombs with May 1st, the International Workers Holiday created in the wake of the Haymarket Affair. The message behind the chosen date was clear. While these bombings failed to kill any of the targets, many people were injured and panic gripped the nation as they awaited the next attack. It would come in June, and this time two Americans would die.

This time the homemade bombs were larger and more effectively crafted. Galleani's anarchist followers enacted this second wave of bombings in eight different American cities and paired them with flyers that declared anarchist intentions to make war with western capitalists. One of these bombs damaged the home of the U.S. Attorney General, Alexander Palmer.

This particular attack almost certainly inspired Palmer to act swiftly and decisively to combat these domestic threats to America. Following his testimony to the House Appropriations Committee in June of 1919, Palmer was granted a 100,000 dollar increase in budgetary funds to investigate political radicals in the United States.

After one of Palmer's early raids, a Federal Judge tossed out a case against three radicals. Palmer tried to utilize a Civil War-era law to prosecute the defendants, but it failed. The accused proposed that free speech, and not violence, were means of transforming the American government. So Palmer adjusted his approach, looking to newly minted immigration statutes to achieve the deportation of naturalized leftists, whether they advocated for violent revolution or not.

Palmer enlisted the help of the Department of Labor in these efforts, as the Labor Secretary of the United States was the only government official eligible to issue warrants and sign deportation orders regarding violations of the Immigration Act of 1918.

In August, Palmer promoted a young J. Edgar Hoover to lead up the General Intelligence Division, a new offshoot of the Bureau of Investigations. The 24-year-old Hoover was now responsible for investigating the inner workings of radical groups within the United States.

Three months later, on the second anniversary of the Bolshevik revolution, the Bureau of Investigation enacted a series of violent, highly publicized raids on The Union of Russian Workers. Palmer's investigators didn't stop at Union members though.

Some of the suspects apprehended by the government officials were only detained because they admitted to being of Russian descent. Others were night school teachers who were guilty of sharing a classroom with suspected radicals. Of the 650 people arrested, only 43 of them were deported.

These raids would have a lasting effect on the contemporary political landscape of the United States. In May of 1920 the American Civil Liberties Union, founded partially in response to the Justice Department's initiatives, published the Report Upon the Illegal Practices of the United States Department of Justice. It shone a light on the unlawful, unconstitutional practices of Palmer's investigations.

The House Rules Committee called Palmer in for another hearing that June, where he accused his critics of harboring treasonous sympathies for revolutionary factions. That same month, a Massachusetts District Court Judge ordered for the release of several defendants indicted after the Palmer Raids. The Judge condemned the Department of Justice's actions and prevented any similar raids.

Due in part to this ruling, Palmer's political future was effectively neutralized and he lost his bid for the Democratic nomination later that year. Anarchist bombings would continue intermittently for twelve more.

The Frankfurt School

Three years after Palmer's failed bid for the Democratic nomination, and thousands of miles away, in post-World War I Germany, Felix Weil founded The Institute for Social Research.

Weil sought to foster new studies into German society through the lens of Marx's ideologies. The Institute would also serve to archive information on early labor movements and the historical phenomena of anti-Semitism.

The turbulent political situation in America was by no means an isolated occurrence. The Frankfurt school proposed that the practice of social theory could not hope to adequately solve the continual clashes between contemporary capitalist governments and the global working classes.

Critical of Marxism, capitalism, and any other ideologies that demanded the adoption of inflexible social structures, the Frankfurt school advocated instead for the use of critical theory in realizing the social development of any given nation-state.

These German critical theorists based their doctrines on the studies of famous intellectuals, like Karl Marx, Sigmund Freud, and Georg Wilhelm Freidrich Hegel. They did not, however, limit themselves to the ideologies and practices of those great minds. Utilizing methods of psychoanalysis, existentialism, and sociology, they blended various themes and philosophies into an overarching rubric of critical thought they believed would bring about positive changes in the world.

Though the institute drew heavily from Marx's works, its ideological stances differ widely from orthodox Marxism, mainly because critical theory is by nature self-critical. As a sociological study, it lends little credence to Marx's ideas about universal truths and the inescapable cycles of human history.

By 1930, Max Horkheimer was named director of The Institute for Social Research. The scholars that Horkheimer recruited would come to be known to history as "The

Frankfurt School". These intellectuals were disheartened by the current political climate of Europe and feared the continued rise of authoritarianism in the west.

To combat this threat, they stressed a need for cultural analysis of western patriarchy, racism, and authoritarianism. According to the Institute, without this analysis, communism could never truly take shape. Without it came the inevitable rise of authoritarian governments.

The Frankfurt School was also concerned with the "mass-culture" phenomena. For most of our shared history, nation-states and their respective cultural evolutions were separated by great geographical distances and physical borders. The theorists believed that the invention and widespread adoption of modern communication technologies had forever transformed the transmission methods of cultural products (such as films, music, art, and literature) and values between one society and another. This new technology served to make the world a much smaller, much more accessible place. Now the public could simply "observe" cultural products instead of actively engaging with each other as in ages past.

The Frankfurt School of philosophy proposed that this new paradigm fostered intellectual apathy among the general public, due to their constant unconscious exposure to mass-produced social, political, and cultural ideologies.

They were critical of the newly emergent consumer culture that the Industrial Revolution had ushered in, and argued that it could only maintain itself through the exploitative means of capitalist systems.

With the rise of the Nazi party in Germany and the advent of fascism throughout the country, the Frankfurt school was forced to uproot its institute. They relocated first to Geneva and eventually to New York City.

Though the German scholars would find sanctuary during American exile, they could not hope to escape the antisemitism that had recently forced them from their homes. They were made to watch helplessly as the horrific genocide of Jews and other minorities began under the Nazis.

These exiled critical theorists couldn't help but compare the atmosphere of 1930's America to that of their beleaguered homeland. In Germany, the Nazis had long ago adopted theories on the causes of revolutions and upheavals in western society. As with the rest of the socio-political issues facing Germany at the time, the Nazis foisted blame squarely on the shoulders of their perceived enemies, the Jewish population.

Some of the earliest examples of Nazi propaganda about Jews originated as a popular conspiracy theory called "cultural Bolshevism" or "Judeo-Bolshevism".

The Nazis described a global cabal of Zionists who were corroding traditional western values by any means necessary. According to Hitler and his cohorts, these hypothetical overlords sought the downfall of Gentile nation-states through subversive practices. They wanted to weaken the genetic purity of native-born Germans and lure them into a position of weakness and subservience. They were not above using emerging technology, art, culture, and political discourse to achieve these aims. The Zionists had formed an unholy alliance with leftist factions and the Nazis blamed the rise of socialism, communism, and anarchism on this secret menace.

Though initially helpless to combat the growing, fascist threat of the Nazi party, the Frankfurt school would eventually play an important role in gathering intelligence reports on Hitler's regime for the Office of Strategic Services. Their perspectives and analysis on Nazism would go on to provide a critical framework for the American government's wartime strategy against the Third Reich. Their work would also provide a detailed plan for the reconstruction of a post-Nazi Germany under a democratic regime.

The Frankfurt School's views on denazification deeply influenced the United States' postwar foreign policy and helped prepare for the notorious Nuremberg Trials. In 1953, twenty years after the Institute for Social Research was forced to relocate, some members of the Frankfurt School were able to return to West Germany.

From Cultural Bolshevism to Cultural Marxism

To most Americans during the early years of the Cold War, the dreaded "Red Menace" was no longer the looming threat it had once been. World War II had forever changed the U.S. labor movement. The demands of early activists were now seen as normal parts of working-class life

The same consumer culture that the Frankfurt School warned against had now successfully taken root across the modern world. The values and ideals of the American ruling class reigned supreme. The doctrines of Marxists, socialists, communists, and other factions were rejected by the public at large and free-market capitalism was the dominant ideology of most developed nations.

Over the ensuing decades, capitalism would prove the most powerful force in solidifying America's position as the preeminent superpower of the modern world. Quality of life began to improve and the strengthening of the American middle class created a whole new world of economic opportunity.

In modern times, certain conservatives have begun to reexamine this era, and according to some, while the western capitalists were celebrating the effective defeat of collectivism, a sinister plot was being hatched right under their noses.

The theory posits that Marxist radicals, well aware of their impending defeat at the hands of capitalists everywhere, began to scheme ways to repackage their philosophies for future generations. These crafty radicals threw themselves into the undertaking and pulled an about-face, turning their critiques from economic systems of control to cultural issues. To those who peddle these conspiracy theories, cultural Marxists still wanted to bring about violent revolutions, but they used culture to enact behavioral conditioning.

Cultural Marxists then began using their new methods of subversion after the groundwork was laid down by the Frankfurt School. They transposed Marx's earlier ideas about the oppressed versus the oppressor into the realm of cultural products, using art, literature, cinema, and radio production to prey on minorities.

Marxists sought to convince these minorities of their victimhood, and turn Americans against each other to sabotage our country from within. This conspiracy theory is very similar to the theory of Cultural Bolshevism except the Jews are replaced with Marxists as the stealthy proprietors of false doctrines, intent on bringing about the destruction of capitalist nations.

Given our nation's history of persecuting leftists, it isn't all that surprising to learn that a theory like that of Cultural Marxism might gain traction in the shared imagination of the American public, even with its roots planted firmly in Nazi Germany.

In the years after World War II, this fear-mongering and political conspiracy would further serve to deepen the many divides in America. These methods are still utilized by the majority of our politicians today, on either side of the aisle.

These divides would define the political and social considerations of the Cold War, leading to one particularly infamous chapter of American history: The Second Red Scare.

Chapter 3: Shades of Red, White, and Blue

Before beginning research for this work, I was unfamiliar with the historical existence of more than one "Red Scare" period in America's past. I was fully aware, however, of the more well-known of these periods.

Most Americans are at least tangentially familiar with the general events of the Second Red Scare in the early 1950s, led up by the notorious Wisconsin Senator, Joseph McCarthy. McCarthy's influence on this era of American history was so great that it will forever bear his namesake in the annals of U.S. history. "McCarthyism" soon became synonymous with undermining or defeating political enemies with baseless attacks on their loyalty to America.

The legislative groundwork for McCarthy's Cold War offensive was laid down by American bureaucrats during the First Red Scare, including the Overton Committee. While the committee was unsuccessful in achieving any real anti-communist reform, its sensational reports played an important role in spurring on the public's fear of radical immigrants. It was only the first of many such committees, all tasked with investigating the rise of political agitators in America.

On May 5th of 1930, a staunchly anti-communist, Republican Congressman, Hamilton Fish III, introduced House Resolution 180. This resolution proposed the establishment of a committee to investigate American citizens and organizations accused of involvement with (or support of) communists in the United States.

Congress decided to permit this, and the Fish Committee was born. Thanks in part to the Fish Committee's recommendations, the Special Committee on Un-American Activities was formed in 1934. This particular iteration was focused on foreign propaganda and how it was used as a tool of subversion, investigating Nazi propaganda and fascist plots to upend the American government.

A year after the Special Committee was disbanded in 1937, the House Committee on Un-American Activities was created, and this time its focus returned to investigating communist influence and activity. That year, the HCUA subpoenaed the head of the Federal Theatre Project, Hallie Flanagan, to stand before them and answer allegations that her organization was crawling with communist radicals.

The Federal Theatre Project was a part of the Works Progress Administration. The WPA was established during the Great Depression as a caveat of FDR's New Deal and the project was created to help provide relief for impoverished theatre workers, artists, writers, and directors. In response to the HCUA's accusations and Flanagan's hour-long testimony before the committee, Congress canceled all federal funding of the FTP in the summer of 1939.

That same year, the committee also subpoenaed George Van Horn Moseley, who they suspected harbored tied to pro-Nazi organizations. Moseley's five-hour testimony claimed that the Jews and the communists of Europe had united in a plot to seize control of the government.

Moseley brought with him one Donald Shea of the American Gentile League. Shea's testimony was stricken from the public record because the HCUA found it too objectionable to include in its dictations.

Democratic Congressman Edward Hart was appointed as the standing body's first chairman. Citing Public Law 601, a legislative mandate from the 79th Congress of the United States, the committee validated its authority to investigate any subversive threats to the country.

In 1946 the HCUA declined to investigate the terrorist activities carried out by the infamous Klu Klux Klan. One of the committee chairs was John Rankin, a white supremacist Democrat from Mississippi After the decision was reached, Rankin was reported to have stated: "After all, the KKK is an old American institution." (Newton, 2020)

In 1948, the HCUA rendered charges of espionage and sedition against one Alger Hiss, a government Lawyer, and State Department official. The basis of these charges came from accusations levied by Elizabeth Bentley, a former Soviet spy who defected in 1945. Bentley claimed dozens of U.S. officials were complicit in Soviet-sponsored espionage against the American government, including Hiss.

The FBI opened an investigation into Bentley's testimony. The officials named were stripped of their jobs so as not to allow for continued access to sensitive government information. As the investigation stretched on into 1947, Congress caught wind of it, and eventually, details were leaked to the press, just in time for the upcoming general election.

In August, the HCUA subpoenaed a senior editor of Time Magazine, Whittaker Chambers. Chambers had renounced the Communist Party a decade earlier. He admitted to participating in the American Communist Underground of the early 1930s. He named Hiss as a comrade. Hiss denied this charge. He asserted that Chambers offered no proof because he had none, because he was making all the charges up.

The committee might have ended their investigation there, but a Republican Congressman from California named Richard Nixon kept pressing Chambers for more information. He suggested to his fellow committee members that Chambers was withholding critical information. Perhaps due to Nixon's dogged efforts, Albert Hiss later admitted to knowing Whittaker Chambers in the 1930s, but he still denied any ties to communism. The committee debated amongst themselves as to whether Hiss or Chambers was trying to deceive them, which of them should be charged with perjury.

Then in November, Chambers provided a smoking gun for the Justice Department. This evidence was hidden inside a pumpkin on his Maryland property. The "Pumpkin Papers" included notes in Hiss' handwriting and images of confidential government materials. Afterward, Hiss was charged with perjury and sentenced to five years imprisonment. Though the FBI's investigation netted plenty of evidence against Hiss, the statute of limitations on his espionage charges had run out.

Hiss' case was highly polarizing at the time. It convinced many more government officials of the importance and usefulness of the committee. Its reach soon stretched far and wide, traveling across the nation to Hollywood, the global epicenter of America's entertainment industry.

In July of 1946, William Wilkerson, one of the founders of The Hollywood Reporter, published a column entitled "*A Vote for Joe Stalin*" which named several high-profile, Hollywood figures as secret Communist sympathizers. This growing list of names would come to be called "Billy's Blacklist". (Baum & Miller, 2012) The HCUA drew from Wilkerson's work and issued subpoenas to various persons in the American entertainment industry.

A group of ten writers and directors called to speak before the committee refused to testify, citing their constitutional right to freedom of speech and assembly. One of the questions they wouldn't answer was the oft-repeated line: "Are you now, or have you ever been, a member of the Communist party?" (*McCarthyism [Ushistory.Org]*, n.d.)

It was soon discovered that members of the Hollywood Ten were card-carrying communist party members. They were eventually found guilty of their charges and were sentenced to a year in jail. As a result of the case, a group of powerful studio executives gathered together to decide on a plan of action going forward. They released a statement to the press condemning the charges levied by Congress, though the accused had not yet been found guilty.

This statement was thereby referred to as the "Waldorf Declaration," referring to the hotel where the executives stayed while devising the press release. The Waldorf Declaration stated, "We will not knowingly employ a Communist or a member of any party or group which advocates the overthrow of the government of the United States by force or by any illegal or unconstitutional methods" (Brianton, 2019).

Surely, a motivating factor for this decision was the public outcry against the Hollywood Ten and possible fears of the HCUA's wrath. Though they knew it might create a terrifying atmosphere, that was a price that these Hollywood powerhouses were willing to pay in the name of national security.

> In pursuing this policy, we are not going to be swayed by hysteria or intimidation from any source. We are frank to recognize that such a policy involves danger and risks. There is the danger of hurting innocent people. There is the risk of creating an atmosphere of fear. Creative work at its best cannot be carried on in an atmosphere of fear. We will guard against this danger, this risk, this fear. (Society of Independent Motion Picture Producers, 2005)

The capitulations of the Waldorf Declaration opened the doors for rampant chaos to blossom in the entertainment industry. The criteria for being blacklisted could be as tangential as attending a political meeting or signing a petition. Blacklisted individuals were shunned by the industry at large and barred from making a living by almost every major film studio.

"Dislodge the Traitors From Every Place"

Joseph McCarthy, who would one day become the face of the Second Red Scare, was born in Grandchute, Wisconsin in 1908. He attended school until the eighth grade. Afterward, McCarthy tried his hand at starting his own chicken business but was left near penniless when disease wiped out his flock.

In 1928, he was working as a clerk at a local grocery store where he was soon promoted to manager. He transferred to Manawa, Washington the next year to take over management duties at a new store. During this time McCarthy enrolled in Little Wolf Highschool and completed four years of curriculum in just nine months. His impressive marks allowed him to begin his secondary education at Milwaukee's Marquette University. After obtaining his law degree, McCarthy opened up a practice in 1935, in Waucapa, Wisconsin. He would eventually join a law firm in Shawano and was named a partner in 1937.

He ran for Shawano District Attorney as a Democrat in 1936 but was defeated. In 1939 McCarthy was elected to the Tenth Judicial Circuit Court which had jurisdiction over Langlade, Shawano, and Outagamie Counties. McCarthy was noted for his work ethic and his fair-minded rulings, he was also sanctioned by the State Supreme Court for abusing his judicial authority by destroying official court records.

Though he ran as a Democrat in 1936, by 1944 McCarthy had switched over to the Republican ticket. That year he challenged Senator Alexander Wiley for the Republican nomination to the Senate, but he lost. When he ran for circuit court judge in 1945, he was duly re-elected to the position. Almost as soon as it ended, McCarthy set about making plans for the senate race of 1946.

He would go on to defeat incumbent Republican Senator Robert La Follette by a small portion of votes. Then, he soundly defeated his Democratic opponent and left Wisconsin for Washington.

Less than four years after his decisive Senate victory, McCarthy gave a historical speech in Wheeling, West Virginia, wherein he claimed to be aware of 205 Communist party members currently working for the U.S. Department of State. McCarthy would soon find himself propelled to a position of fame, power, and respect after his speech began to garner extensive media attention.

Nine days after his initial salvo, on February 20th of 1950, McCarthy went on to address the Senate, where he would repeat his accusations to his peers and colleagues. Though the Senator provided no real evidence for his narrative, the Senate never-the-less ordered a full investigation into McCarthy's damning claims.

In the summer of 1950, Congress could find no grounds for the validity of McCarthy's charges. This did not deter him. He would continue to make accusations of communists within the government.

In 1953, Truman was replaced by Republican candidate Dwight Eisenhower. Eisenhower was not a fan of McCarthy or his policies, but he was afraid to split the loyalties of the party, so he worked behind the scene to neutralize the Senator instead of openly attacking him in the press. For his part, McCarthy went so far as to accuse Eisenhower of harboring communists within his administration.

Despite his differences with Republican leadership, McCarthy became chairman of the Senate Committee on Government Operations and its investigative subcommittee. He used this position to initiate the investigation of the Army Signal Corps but was unsuccessful at uncovering any sort of spy ring or Communist plot. During his investigation, McCarthy's treatment of General Ralph Zwicker led many of McCarthy's former supporters to denounce him.

With time, this opposition snowballed, until in 1954 CBS News premiered Edward R. Murrow's "See It Now" news package, which served as a scathing indictment on McCarthy and his methods in hunting down suspected Communists.

Afterward, the U.S. Army released a special report which detailed claims that McCarthy, along with his legal aide Roy Cohn, had previously exerted pressure on the Army to provide another McCarthy aid with preferential treatment after he was drafted. McCarthy reacted by making his claims that the Army was using these charges as a means of political extortion.

This dispute was broadcast live on American national television in the spring and summer of 1954. These broadcasts led to the tarnishing of McCarthy's public image. The climax of these hearings came when McCarthy was asked a question by Joseph Welch, who served as the Army's chief counsel. He queried McCarthy: "Have you no sense of decency, sir, at long last? Have you no sense of decency?" (Appleton Public Library Wisconsin, n.d.)

McCarthy's reputation would never recover from this public fiasco, and his investigative hearings netted only inconclusive results. That August, a Senate committee was commissioned to investigate whether McCarthy should be censured for his actions.

By September, the committee's report was presented to the Senate. In it, they labeled the Wisconsin Senator's behavior while he was acting chairman to be "reprehensible" and "inexcusable". These findings drove the Senate to pass a resolution condemning McCarthy for abuses of power. The vote passed by a margin of 67-22. (Appleton Public Library Wisconsin, n.d.)

McCarthy, who had long been a heavy drinker, began to increase his levels of alcohol consumption until they reached dangerous heights. In April of 1957, he was admitted to the hospital due to a liver ailment. He died early the next month in Washington, on May 2nd, 1957, of acute hepatitis.

McCarthy's Legacy

Two years before McCarthy's death, Supreme Court Justice William O. Douglas published an article in the New York Times entitled "The Black Fear of Silence." In it, Justice Douglas wrote a stirring commentary on the mass hysteria that gripped the American population during the Second Red Scare.

He blamed the unreasonable fervor of the anti-Communist movement, in part, for making America a more intolerant and bigoted country. In Douglas' eyes, our crippling fear of foreigners and outsiders had paralyzed us into the monotony of stagnancy and orthodoxy.

To solve this problem, Douglas called upon Americans to embrace the free exchange of thought and expression, which he believed was crucial if we were to evolve economically, politically, and socially. Our inability to accept values and ideologies that conflicted with our own was holding us back, weakening our chances at a brighter future.

The introduction to Douglas' article prefaces his concerns:

> There is an ominous trend in this nation. We are developing tolerance only for the orthodox point of view on world affairs, intolerance for new or different approaches. Orthodoxy normally has stood in the path of change. Orthodoxy was always the stronghold of the status quo, the enemy of new ideas- (Douglas, 1952)

His view of contemporary America sounds eerily similar to the atmosphere of Nazi Germany, as well as that of the First Red Scare, and Tsarist Russia, and Victorian England, and pre-Unification Germany, and Renaissance Italy, and ancient Mesopotamia.

Marxism was created as a philosophical approach to answer why humanity, in all its many societal iterations, seems to follow these cycles without fail. Marxists hold to the notion that the government of any given nation should evolve with the current needs of its people.

Our government has historically infringed upon its people's rights to freedom of speech and expression. It has seen fit to do so by stoking fears about "radical" political elements, to stamp out even the perceived threat of leftist thought and theory.

The ruling classes benefit from this fearmongering. Whether they are behind it is a question for another book, and many better authors than I have already tackled it in great detail in the past. You can even read what Karl Marx has to say about it if you so choose.

Looking back at McCarthyism and the Second Red Scare, one inevitably begins to think about the impact this tumultuous period had on American politics. It caused tangible consequences that reverberate into the modern day; but what about the things that didn't happen because of it?

What workers were not organized into unions? What works of art, literature, cinema, and theater were never created? What social reforms were never constructed, to better the lives of American citizens?

One must also ponder what kind of toll the Red Scare must have wrought on the American left. The aims of our government have proven successful, at least in regards to wiping communism off of the metaphorical playing field. They pushed our political spectrum further to the right, making moderate liberals look like the "extreme" end of the new left. No longer was it the Marxists and socialists labeled as fringe extremists, but the moderate reformers.

McCarthyism forced the labor movement to change its focus from externalized organizing to internal disagreements about political ideologies. The goals of FDR's New Deal were never fully achieved due to this post-war shift. One of the New Deal's social reforms, nationalized health insurance, was never realized either. The United States is still the only country in the developed world without a system of universal healthcare.

After McCarthy's reign of terror ended, opposition to American Cold War policy had been so thoroughly identified with communists that citizens could no longer seek to challenge policy decisions without courting suspicions of "Un-American" activity. Until the early 1960s, criticism of America's role on the geopolitical stage was, for all intents and purposes, nonexistent. It would take the combined forces of the American Civil Rights movement, a massive wave of antiwar sentiment during the Vietnam War era, and the advent of the counterculture of the late 60s to bring about an end to this complacency.

Even once the anti-communist outcry died down, the antidemocratic measures used by McCarthy and his contemporaries remained. From the FBI's infamous COINTELPRO program to President Nixon's Watergate debacle, to the Iran-Contra scandals of the 80s, McCarthy's legacy provides our government with an effective shield against the consequences of their own wrongdoings.

The idea that ensuring national security was more important than constitutional rights and freedoms has rendered the American working class nearly powerless against a myriad of illegalities and corruptions. It is a fair argument that the Second Red Scare did more to bring about the decline of American values than any facet of the dreaded "Red Menace" ever did.

Chapter 4: How to Spin a Century

Harry S. Truman knew the difference between socialism and communism.

He was one of the main participants in setting the geopolitical stage for the Cold War era and an avid opponent of the communist party. Still, Truman recognized the positive impacts that socialism could have on the lives of his citizens.

To Marxists, socialism is the best system to replace the barbarous capitalist systems which disproportionately benefit the ruling classes. To Truman, socialism was a tool best used by democratic societies to curtail the worst excesses of the free market and ensure a better quality of life for all Americans.

President Truman also served as Vice President to his predecessor, Franklin Roosevelt. Contemporary Republicans were quite fond of lobbing accusations of socialism at the Roosevelt administration, though these smears did little to abate his popularity among the American people at large. Amid the Great Depression of the late 30s, when our country was experiencing never before seen levels of unemployment, homelessness, poverty, and economic stagnation, it was to this American public that Roosevelt turned to combat these struggles.

During his famous "Fireside Chats" the President shared visions of a brighter future for his people over the radio waves, and this strategy helped him pass one of the most complex and comprehensive government legislations known to the modern world: the New Deal. His Republican opponents found it hard to argue against these popular policies, as they greatly benefitted the working classes, and to stand against them could cost them their careers. But after FDR's death, and following the historic rise of the Soviet Union, they found a new way of discrediting the progressive, liberal ideas of the quintessential reformist. They turned to dishonest and subversive policies of their own, to combat the dishonest, subversive policies they claimed were utilized by the opposition.

That opposition ranged from socialists to communists, to anarchists, to fascists, to postmodernists and beyond. It didn't matter what the actual beliefs of these political doctrines were, only that these hypocritical politicians could use them to represent an all-encompassing boogeyman; a grand, unified conspiracy to bring down democracy and the western way of life, once and for all.

A month before Dwight Eisenhower won the Presidential election of 1952, Truman spoke on the subject of the American version of this age-old racket in Syracuse New York:

> Socialism is a scare word they have hurled at every advance the people have made
> in the last 20 years. Socialism is what they called public power. Socialism is what
> they called Social Security. Socialism is what they called farm price supports.
> Socialism is what they called bank deposit insurance. Socialism is what they
> called the growth of free and independent labor organizations. Socialism is their
> name for almost anything that helps all the people. When the Republican
> candidate inscribes the slogan 'Down with Socialism' on the banner of his 'great
> crusade,' that is really not what he means at all. What he really means is 'Down
> with Progress – down with Franklin Roosevelt's New Deal,'...That's all he means.
> (Truman, 1952)

At the outset of his Presidency, Truman hoped for peace between the Soviet Union and
the United States, but the policies and agendas of his Russian contemporary, Josef
Stalin, soon made this impossible.

Stalin used underhanded tactics like spreading propaganda, creating an abusive sect of
Russian secret police, sedition, and espionage to establish his control over the Soviet
Union. By 1946 Stalin's Russia was eager to expand its reach, and establish itself as the
dominant power in the post-war era. Suddenly, the socialist inspirations that helped to
craft the foundation of FDR's New Deal were seen as tools of evil. This strategy, to attack
the ideological origins of leftist policies and to turn citizens against each other, is one
that Republicans never abandoned.

The Greatest Delusion

What do you think about when you hear the names of Thomas Paine? Or Adam Smith?
What about Ralph Waldo Emerson or Nathaniel Hawthorne?

What comes to mind when someone mentions Francis Bellamy, Albert Einstein, W.E.B
Dubois, Pablo Picasso, or Nelson Mandela? How about Helen Keller? Martin Luther
King Junior? What if I told you that these people were all supporters of socialist ideas?

It might surprise you, but we have socialist ideas to thank for our public roads and
infrastructures. The highways that millions of Americans travel on daily are funded by
taxpayers. The police departments of this country are taxpayer-funded programs that
were built on socialism. The police are charged with serving and protecting entire
communities, not just the individuals within them that pay taxes. If they were privatized
and run using purely capitalist principles, we would all pay fees every time we needed
the police to aid us.

One of America's most successful exports, warfare, is a socialist program. The vast majority of taxes we pay to the U.S. Government are used to wage wars overseas. Private companies don't have the power or resources to engage in their wars, as they would under a purely capitalist government.

Then there's Social Security, a system we all pay taxes towards, that acts as a social safety net for elderly Americans once they've retired or are unable to work due to old age. Though many members of Congress like to give damning warnings about the evils of government-regulated healthcare, they are all the while covered by taxpayer-funded, government-run health care plans. We quite literally shell out the money for their health care costs, while they proclaim their system of choice is socialism and should be avoided at all costs.

Private insurance companies pay for government officials' political campaigns and, as such, our representatives are beholden to push their agendas over legislation that would benefit the average, working-class American. It wasn't until the 1980s, however, that this hypocrisy became public policy with the election of perhaps the most beloved conservative politician of our time, President Ronald Reagan.

"A Nation Gone Under"

In 1961, Ronald Reagan gave a radio address concerning the threat that socialized medicine posed to the American people. He predicted that the passage of Medicare would curtail our rights and freedoms, though its proponents claimed it was an act of altruism and humanitarianism. In his address Regan warned:

> All of us can see what happens: Once you establish the precedent that the government can determine a man's working place and his working methods, determine his employment, from here it's a short step to all the rest of socialism -- to determining his pay, and pretty soon your son won't decide when he's in school, where he will go, or what they will do for a living. He will wait for the government to tell him where he will go to work and what he will do. (*American Rhetoric Online Speech Bank, 1961*)

Despite his dire prophecies, Medicare eventually passed and 1960s America was still free to decide where they would live, work, and pursue their happiness.

Regan was not alone in his condemnation of Medicare. Of our elected representatives 17 Republican senators voted against its passage, along with seven Democratic senators. In the House, 68 Republicans and 48 Democrats stood in opposition. Though he had yet to begin his political career, Reagan would eventually get the chance to undermine

Medicare in ways his acting career had never allowed. He was elected to office in 1980, 19 years after his anti-socialist radio address aired.

In the first few years of his presidency, his administration drastically cut Medicare spending by more than eighteen percent. Federal funding for maternal and child healthcare was reduced by eighteen percent. The Department of Health and Human Services saw its budget slashed by twenty-five percent, eliminating many public health initiatives. The effects of his policies were far-far reaching and would cause widespread suffering for the American populace.

During Reagan's administration, most Public Health Service Hospitals (which sent doctors to impoverished rural and urban areas) were shuttered. More than two 200 community health centers were closed. Six hundred thousand American citizens lost their Medicaid coverage. A million more people lost their food stamps. WIC, which provides low-income pregnant women and children with formula and healthy food, could no longer afford to cover almost two-thirds of its former beneficiaries. Over Reagan's two terms in office, 309 rural, and 294 urban hospitals were forced to close. Between 1982 and 1978, cases of unintended pregnancy rose by almost eight percent.

The amount of uninsured Americans exploded. At the outset of Reagan's second term, fifteen percent of the population was without any form of health insurance, and those who had once turned to Medicare experienced a rapid decline in their overall health, and the health of their communities. By 1991, more than thirty-four million individuals went without health insurance because they simply couldn't afford it. In "A Time For Choosing," Reagan's famous conservative manifesto, he spoke to the 1964 Republican National Convention. In it, he announced, "No one in this country should be denied medical care for lack of funds." (Roy, 2018)

But twenty years later, Reagan proved that this belief would not craft his policies on American healthcare. Though his predictions for the future of Medicare inevitably proved false, he never turned away from his decades-long crusade against it. Under Reagan, private insurance corporations began to integrate themselves into the hospital system, which had previously been a decentralized structure. Because of Reagan's economic healthcare policies, there was a historical shift towards the privatization and corporatization of healthcare. So who benefited from these policies?

Regan's administration wasn't able to free up any budgetary spending, even with these massive cuts. Poor Americans were turned away in droves with no recourse for their illnesses and injuries. It would seem that the only real winners in this whole debacle were private, American insurance providers. Like many of Reagan's policy plans, it was the wealthy who benefited, not the average American.

Perhaps we shouldn't be surprised, given that his original campaign against "socialized medicine" was funded and sponsored by the American Medical Association. Reagan's radio address was a part of their campaign to oppose government-paid health insurance for the elderly.

A year after he gave the address, Reagan would join the Republican party and his first foray into politics would eventually lead him to the highest office in the land, where he would further legislation that benefited organizations like the AMA while leaving millions of American's without a place to turn regarding their health, their families health, and the health of their communities at large. Despite this, Ronald Reagan is considered a hero of the Republican party, and his years in office would shape conservative ideology for decades to come.

In particular, Reagan's opposition to "socialized healthcare" has had dire consequences on the health and wellbeing of our nation and the party Reagan helped to redefine. In September of 2007, 46 years after Reagan's anti-socialist broadcast, presidential candidate Mitt Romney commented on then-rival Hillary Clinton's proposed health care agenda. "It's a European-style socialized medicine plan," he said. "That's where it leads, and that's the wrong direction for America." (Morning Edition, 2007) Modern Republicans have often made similarly dire warnings about the Affordable Care Act, President Barack Obama's legislative attempt to overhaul the United States healthcare system.

This didn't stop the ACA from passing, and the polarizing bill has yet to usher in a new age of socialism or socialized medicine. That fact hasn't stopped conservatives from brandishing the S world at every opportunity, trying to bolster support for their agenda of repealing the law. As we've seen, this fiery crusade is an old ploy. Yet none of their apocalyptic promises have come to fruition.

Instead, the insurance companies, and their billion-dollar campaign contributions, keep an iron grip on America's healthcare industry. They are aided by complicit politicians, who continue to dangle leftist boogeymen, to distract us from this grim reality.

Chapter 5: Rouse the Cowards

Two years into Donald Trump's presidential term, his Council of Economic Advisers published a seventy-two-page report entitled "The Opportunity Costs of Socialism", a capitalist rebuke of growing calls for redistributive government policies. Strangely enough, the CEA chose the publishing date to recognize the 200th anniversary of Karl Marx's birth. It warns of the dangers that America's free market, and our democracy, will face if socialists are allowed to seize power.

In one excerpt, the report explains that "-the recipients of Christmas gifts sometimes value the gifts less than they cost the giver, as exemplified by Christmas sweaters that are never taken out of the closet to be worn." (The Council of Economic Advisors, 2018) This passage is supposed to be a metaphor for the theory of mixed value. The report likewise asserts that "-owning and operating a pickup truck costs the average worker in a Nordic country substantially more than it costs the average American worker" to try and persuade readers that capitalism is the only system that offers true economic freedom. It points to famines and food shortages in Maoist China and Stalinist Russia as proof of capitalism's superiority, even though both of those governments were openly communist. It is a strange and rambling work that offers no real substance or depth. Rather than trying to present me with facts and let me make up my mind, the CEA's screed served only to fill me with a bizarre sense of secondhand embarrassment. And it is in no way the worst example of Republican absurdity in recent memory. Not even close.

"The Great American Story"

If you listen to most mainstream politicians and pundits, you might believe that socialists or Marxists, or anarchists are poised and ready to strike at any moment, ready to ruin the American values that used to make us great.

Sarah Jones, a self-proclaimed socialist, and a reporter for New York Magazine wrote about the paranoia and fear rising within the Republican party in August of 2020. She stated:

> If one experience unites the American left across generational and factional divides, it's losing. I wish that were not the case, but facts are facts and I must admit them. I am a socialist, and I am a loser. Do we have a socialist nominee for

president? We do not. Did we even get a social democrat? Also no. Did we get Medicare for All in the Democratic Party platform? We did not. Delegates, including several union leaders, shot it down. A smattering of comrades in Congress and various state legislatures provides a reason for hope, but it is also not the same thing as a mass movement for socialism. (S. Jones, 2020)

Jones is prefacing an article that details the events of last year's Republican National Convention, where the great myth of imminent, socialist destruction was alive and well among the nation's most popular conservative public figures. Seeing as this was three months away from the general election, the Republican politicians, celebrities, and special guests spent the majority of their time during the nominating trying to hold up Donald Trump as the country's only hope against the evils of Marxists, who wanted to steal the rights and freedoms of God-fearing Americans from coast-to-coast.

The Republican National Committee opted not to use the convention to update their party platform as was the traditional practice. Instead, they recycled the same platform used in 2016, focusing the entirety of their party loyalty on the idea of Trump as a conservative savior, ready to turn back the leftist hoards at the gates.

Nikki Haley, a two-term governor of South Carolina and early Trump critic, turned Ambassador to the UN, focused on Trump's Democratic opponents, Vice President Joe Biden and Senator Kamala Harris. "Their vision for America is socialism," Haley warned, "and we know that socialism has failed everywhere." Though Haley resigned from the position in 2018, she remained supportive of the Trump Administration and went so far as to call Donald Trump a friend. "Joe Biden and the socialist Left," Haley predicted, "would be a disaster for our economy." Haley would eventually go on to defend Trump's conduct after his baseless claims of electoral fraud led to an insurrection in the capital in January of 2021. Kimberly Guilfoyle, a former Fox News personality, and national chair of the Trump Victory Finance Committee, also warned voters about the dangers of a Joe Biden win in November. "Biden, Harris, and their socialist comrades will fundamentally change this nation. This election is a battle for the soul of America. Your choice is clear."

Donald Trump Jr, the President's eldest son, went one step further than Guilfoyle in his rhetorical efforts. "Joe Biden and the radical Left are also now coming for our freedom of speech and want to bully us into submission." Matt Gaetz, a scandal-prone Floridian Congressman, leveled complaints about "woketopians" and claimed they would "disarm you, empty the prisons, lock you in your home, and invite MS-13 to live next door. And the defunded police aren't on their way."(Institute for Public Affairs, 2020)

Joe Biden and Kamala Harris are both centrist, establishment Democrats, neither of whom could be considered liberal, let alone leftist, as far as today's political spectrum is concerned. In September of 2020, Biden gave an interview in Wisconsin while on the campaign trail."I beat the socialist," Biden said "That's how I got elected. That's how I got the nomination. Do I look like a socialist? Look at my career — my whole career. I am not a socialist."(Sherman, 2020)

America is Berning

In February of 2020, the former Republican Governor of Wisconsin, Scott Walker, Tweeted out his opinions on Senator Bernie Sanders, stating, "Bernie is a Communist who admires Communist dictators and he should never be President of the United States of America."(Litke, 2020) In actuality, Bernie is a self-described Democratic Socialist, which is a far cry from a Marxist. Some of his proposed policies are not socialist or even progressive.

Sanders supports Isreal, whereas Marxists typically condemn this government believing the Israelis are committing genocide against the Palestinians. He has also denoted foreign workers as threats to our working class, not as allies in the global struggle against capitalism.

He voted for the use of blockades and sanctions against Iraq during the Gulf War, which Marxists would consider an act of support for U.S. Imperialism. Sanders also voted for NATO's war in the former Yugoslavia in 1999 and in favor of invading Afghanistan in 2001.

Though many of Sander's visions for the American people draw heavily from many different leftist ideologies, the essence of his political career can be distilled down to one idea. Senator Sanders believes that progressive means will bring about the realization of working-class demands in America's capitalist superstructure. Marxist socialists vehemently disagree. Sanders has no intention of leading his "revolution" from a Marxist lens of thought. He is at best a reformer, trying to find ways to improve our social welfare in the suffocating environment of our capitalist, free-market economy.

His goals are admirable and welcomed by millions of working-class Americans, such as free college education, breaking up big banking interests, and fostering higher levels of economic equality. Sanders does not shy away from regularly addressing subjects like union rights, systemic racism, abortion rights, and equality for minorities across the country. He believes he can help put a stop to our nation's woes and achieve his goals, by heading up a political revolution.

To his credit, Sanders is a master in uniting Americans from all different walks of life to create political change. But to Marxists, Sanders is simply a harbinger of bourgeois democracy, wherein the working classes are only given the illusion of choice, the illusion of power, to maintain the hegemony of the ruling classes.

Bernie's idea of political revolution would not change the essential makeup of the state. For Marxists, overthrowing our capitalist system of government and restructuring our entire economy, are essential steps in the emancipation of the working classes.

In a speech addressed to the National Committee for Independent Political Action, Bernie once said,

> Yes, it is true that as a result of the tremendous political ignorance in this country created by the schools and the media, there are many people who do not know the difference between 'socialism' and 'communism.' Yes, on more than one occasion, I have been told to 'go back to Russia.' But, if we maintain a strong position on civil liberties, express our continued opposition to authoritarianism and the concept of the one-party state, I am confident that the vast majority of the people will understand that there is nothing incompatible between socialism and democracy. That has been the case in Vermont and I believe, with proper effort, that it can be the case nationally. Further, given the fact that in Burlington we have almost doubled voter turnout and have significantly increased citizen participation, it is very hard for our opponents to argue that we are not 'democratic.' (Kruse, 2015)

No matter if you disagree with Sanders' platform or not, the evidence is clear that he does not represent the Marxist strong man that Republicans would have voters believe. In a March 2020 interview, a Public Square Magazine writer named Arthur Peña was interviewed by his colleague, Jacob Hess. Peña, a self-professed Marxist, spoke of his disappointment in Bernie Sanders as a candidate:

> For me, as a Marxist, those three words—"Marxist, socialist, communist"—are largely synonymous (though sometimes distinguished one from the other in important ways). I consider myself a Marxist, and therefore also a socialist, and also a communist. But, as you probably have gathered by now, what those words mean to me have very little in common with what they probably mean to you (for example, "communism" to me refers to a distant future condition of society in which all coercive State power has 'withered away'!) So, from the point of view of my definitional universe, I wish Bernie were (more of) a Marxist! (Hess, 2021)

Chapter 6: "But What About...?"

With the growing popularity of socialist ideologies and legislation in our country, those who oppose their implementation have been forced to find new ways of debating against them. Factions with a vested interest in opposing the left seem to have a fixation on countries perceived to be "winners" and "losers" under the labels of Marxism, socialism, and communism.

In my experience, when you try to explain how those policies do not directly line up with the aims and goals of modern American socialists, many conservatives will accuse you of utilizing the "No True Scotsman" fallacy. The No True Scotsman fallacy refers to an example of an "ad hoc rescue", which comes about when an individual is presented with information or evidence that contradicts a dearly held personal belief or value. Said individual is more likely to grasp at variables and exceptions in response to factual information, to justify their refusal to denounce a belief or value.

Let's say, for example, Individual 1 argues that all Scotsmen are good singers. Individual 2 responds by providing an example of a Scotsman they both know, who is an objectively terrible singer. Individual 1, then insists that this is only proof of the fact that their mutual friend is no true Scotsman.

"Glory to the Brave People"

In 2019, Fox News published the second in a series of articles on the dangers of socialism in our government. The piece was entitled, "Democrats now pushing many of the same socialist policies that destroyed Venezuela." In it, they claim, "At the heart of Venezuela's collapse is a laundry list of socialist policies that have decimated its economy." (MacLeod, 2019)

The New York Times published an article that year that sounds very similar. "Venezuela is a socialist catastrophe. In the age of AOC, the lesson must be learned again...socialism never works," (Spielberger, 2018) A year before that, the aforementioned CEA report released by the Trump administration mentioned Venezuela fifty-two times, citing it as evidence of socialism's pitfalls and the opposing virtues of capitalism.

Chávez was elected in 1998. His victory was a modern testament to America's decades-long tradition of political interference in the region, domestic turmoil within the country, and the colloquial "oil curse" that seemed to loom over the Venezuelan people.

In the 1950s at the height of the Second Red Scare, the United States threw its support behind Marcos Pérez Jiménez, a staunchly anti-communist leader whose militant regime was sympathetic to the agendas of foreign oil companies. Jiménez was overthrown in 1958, and the ensuing decade was one of economic prosperity and bitter political struggles for Venezuela. The former would come to a halt in the late 70s, while the latter would completely upend the country's political future.

Carlos Andrés Pérez nationalized the Venezuelan petroleum industry in 1976, and his time as president witnessed the nation's over-reliance on oil as their main economic output. By the late '80s, during Pérez's second term, Venezuela had incurred huge amounts of debt due to drastically reduced oil prices.

Pérez was impeached in 1993 and replaced by Rafael Caldera. Caldera would go on to lose his bid for re-election in 1998, a casualty of Hugo Chávez's infectious populism. The charismatic figurehead diverted the profits of the national oil industry, redistributing them amongst his allies and using them to fund his chosen social programs.

Though Chávez was popular, his policies led to gross mismanagement of government power and his administration was rife with corruption. Chávez had long neglected the nation's infrastructure concerns and by the end of his time as president, the country's oil output had sharply declined. The legacy of Chávismo is one of centralized power and militant rule, meaning that it was in no way a reflection of socialist doctrines and value systems. Even if the ruling government claims to stand for socialist values, if their actions contradict the tenets of the philosophy, how can they justify a wholesale condemnation of it?

"Thou Ancient, Thou Free"

Republicans aren't the only group that contributes to the myriad of misconceptions surrounding socialism. They are not the only players in the eternal game of "winners" and "losers" of modern political discourse. In the same way that conservatives point to Venezuela as the prime example of socialist failure, many American leftists point to Sweden as the prime example of socialist success.

Unlike the Soviet Union, the People's Republic of China, or many other examples of countries that have leftist governing bodies, Sweden is a beacon of democracy and a non-threatening example of what socialism can achieve. But in the same way that America is not wholly capitalist, Sweden is not wholly socialist.

The Nordic system does not exclusively adhere to strict socialist principles in the manner that we understand them. Swedish citizens live and work under a mixed economy, like most developed nations in the west. Sweden's government in particular has been heavily influenced by European neoliberalism since the 90s.

At that point, market-based solutions were introduced into a highly regulated Swedish economic model. Before these solutions were put into effect, during the post-war decades, economic planning had been the dominant method of choice for promoting Sweden's economic growth. They turned to the real-world profits the country could net from the free market and redistributed parts of it for various social programs. The Swedes did not, however, take so much money as to endanger wealth creation.

Sweden boasts a public pension system, their public services are faithfully funded thanks to the help of relatively high tax rates. Free trade is King in Sweden and most of the risks are shared equally amongst most of the citizens, which lessens that risk on any one individual. Sweden also places a relatively high tax burden on its citizen's shoulders. Their taxation rates are fairly flat, which means even lower-income households end up paying higher levels of taxes than the majority of progressive systems in the west.

Though the unswerving efforts of the Swedish working classes garnered many concessions from the highest levels of Nordic society, the corporations of Sweden still enjoy a free-market paradise. In Sweden, capitalism plays just as big a role as socialism in the formation and cultivation of economic and social policy.

No one who mislabels Sweden as a socialist utopia can hope to cry foul when someone they disagree with uses the same methodology to justify their points of view. Discussing the merits of the Nordic system is one thing, subverting their true nature is a pitiful show of bad faith.

If you want to successfully argue on behalf of leftist principles, the most powerful weapons in your arsenal are the truth and a healthy dash of critical thinking skills. They'll take you a lot further than naive or disingenuous claims about Sweden's status as a socialist paradise.

Ignorance is the Enemy

In 1886, the best-selling author and world-famous orator Frederick Douglass gave an address to a crowd in Washington D.C. The speech was given to commemorate the twenty-fourth anniversary of the Emancipation Proclamation in the United States.

Born Frederick Augustus Washington Bailey in 1818, he was the son of a slave named Harriet Bailey and an unknown white father. His mother died when he was seven and he would only see her a handful of times before that. He never learned his father's identity. Douglas was primarily raised by his mother's parents and his aunt.

A year after Harriet's death, the eight-year-old boy was sent to Baltimore, where he was put to work for a ship carpenter. The man's name was Hugh Auld, and during this period the young Douglass learned to read and write. It was in Baltimore that he discovered abolition: the possibility of freedom. Later in his life, Douglass admitted that it was this trip to Baltimore which inevitably "opened the gateway...to all" of his "subsequent prosperity" (Public Broadcasting Service, n.d.).

In September of 1838, Frederick escaped Maryland and traveled north into New York City. He would soon settle in New Bedford, Massachusetts with a new bride and a new name: Frederick Douglass. During his storied career, he would go down in history as one of America's most accomplished writers and orators.

In 1886, Douglass issued a warning to his fellow Americans, a warning about the existence of a conspiracy. Not a conspiracy *theory,* but the more traditional definition of a secret plot crafted to achieve unlawful or harmful ends. Douglas declared, "Where justice is denied, where poverty is enforced, where ignorance prevails, and where any one class is made to feel that society is an organized conspiracy to oppress, rob, and degrade them, neither persons nor property will be safe." (Douglass, 1886)

He describes a familiar scenario in which political and social institutions are beholden to certain subgroups of people, thereby leading these institutions to oppress any others in regards to property, justice, and poverty. Douglass points out that when this scenario unfolds, it endangers the security of all. For when certain members of society are not protected, no one is truly safe. The overarching conditions of oppression do not lend themselves to fair order and will consistently breed resistance and revolution.

Douglass was in no way a supporter of socialism or the emergent philosophies of his contemporary Karl Marx. He was a proponent of the ideology that would come to be known as classical liberalism. Douglass was concerned with racial equality, inherent rights, and a free labor system. He was especially concerned with the right of an individual to own property. But even Douglass conceded:

> If there is no struggle, there is no progress. Those who profess to favor freedom, yet deprecate agitation, are men who want crops without plowing up the ground.

They want rain without thunder and lightning. They want the ocean without the awful roar of its many waters. Power concedes to nothing without a demand. It never did and it never will. (BLACKPAST, 2019)

Though his ideas about freedom were very different from Marx's, they both agreed that action, and sometimes violent action, was needed to capably fight against the conspiracy of class warfare and assure liberty for every person, not just those with all the power.

It is not a matter of Republican or Democrat, left or right, conservative or liberal. It is a matter of behavioral conditioning, and in the wrong hands, these powerful tools can lead to civil war, the loss of human rights, authoritarianism, and destruction. Conspiracy theories can satiate that distant feeling that something just isn't right about our accepted status-quo, if only for a moment. It is only a balm, a distraction, a clever illusion.

In truth, these theories are merely crumbs from a heavily laden table, where the real knowledge is found, and the real power as well. When interest in a conspiracy theory is separated from critical thought, when it is stripped clean of any factual legitimacy, when it is believed without a second thought as the absolute truth, that is when conspiracy theories begin to breed fanaticism and zealotry. That is when they can be used to perpetuate the worst crimes possible against humanity.

In 1955, the University of Chicago Press published *They Thought They Were Free: The Germans, 1933-45* by Milton Sanford Mayer. The book was a look back into the lives of ten ordinary Germans under Hitler's Third Reich. All of them were members of the Nazi party. Mayer shares the story of a Jewish man riding in a German streetcar. Surprisingly, he was reading the Volkischer Beobachter, a daily newspaper produced and sold by the Nazis,

> A non-Jewish acquaintance sits down next to him and says, "Why do you read the Beobachter?" "Look," says the Jew, "I work in a factory all day. When I get home, my wife nags me, the children are sick, and there's no money for food. What should I do on my way home, read the Jewish newspaper? 'Pogrom in Romania' 'Jews Murdered in Poland.' 'New Laws against Jews.' No, sir, a half-hour a day, on the streetcar, I read the Beobachter. 'Jews the World Capitalists,' 'Jews Control Russia,' 'Jews Rule in England.' That's me they're talking about. A half-hour a day I'm somebody. Leave me alone, friend. (Mayer, 2021)

Conspiracy theories about Jewish people have been present in western culture since at least the Middle Ages. By the 20th century, a new era of modern history ushered in a new explanation for how Jews were ruining Europe and the world over. According to the Third Reich, the Jews were now playing puppet masters to the Bolsheviks in Russia and exerting their power through means of cultural subversion and shadow governments.

Large numbers of Europeans came to believe that the unlikely Bolshevik victory could not be explained away so easily as a straightforward historical occurrence. It had to be a part of some far-reaching scheme, some nefarious plot.

And so a new term was coined "Judeo-Bolshevism" or "cultural Bolshevism." Over time, the theory began to pick up steam all over Europe. Stories of postwar communist uprisings were blamed on Jews, who were attempting to crack the very foundations of Christian Europe by bathing the continent in the blood of revolution after revolution.

While it is true that several early 20th century Jews found a home within radical leftist movements, and Jewish people were more well-represented among communist leadership, most Jewish leftists considered their heritages more an accident of birth than a pillar of identity. In his book *A Specter Haunting Europe: The Myth of Judeo-Bolshevism*, author Paul Hanebrink writes, "As they turned to Communism, all broke with the Jewish milieu of their grandfathers, some with a twinge of regret, others with a feeling of liberation." (Hanebrink, 2020)

In actuality, only six out of the Bolshevik leaders of the triumphant faction were Jewish. In time, most Jewish Bolsheviks were purged from the party by Stalin. Despite these indisputable facts, Judeo-Bolshevism and cultural-Bolshevism were used as blank canvases for Europeans to exercise their blood-red fear and paranoia. Hanebrink goes so far as to claim that "Judeo-Bolshevism made Adolf Hitler." It proved a veritable firebrand in Hitler's rhetorical arsenal and was able to combine two cultural "others", the Jews and the Russians, into potent fear-mongering. "The idea of Judeo-Bolshevism was crucial to the genesis of the Final Solution," Hanebrink surmises.

Joseph Goebbels, Hitler's chief propagandist, once said,

> It was the Jew who discovered Marxism. It is the Jew who for decades past has endeavored to stir up world revolutions through the medium of Marxism. It is the Jew who is today at the head of Marxism in all the countries of the world. Only in the brain of a nomad who is without nation, race, and country could this Satanism have been hatched. (Bytwerk, n.d.)

Within far-right factions the world over, this long tradition of linking leftist philosophy with the Jewish "menace" is alive and well. It has become irrevocably entwined with the modern conspiracy theory of cultural Marxism.

Order Out of Chaos

If you seek to identify a wannabe dictator, first decide whether they are willing to undermine and manipulate language. Those who insist on recycling the same misidentified terms over and over again have no moral rigor, nor do they have a defensible position on which to stand. Anyone who seeks to persuade you to stop thinking and start blindly accepting is seldom looking out for your best interests.

They don't care if their arguments hinge on falsehoods and omissions; they seek to frighten people into hating and fearing anyone they label with their redefined words. Conditioning them to attack whatever political enemy needs dispatching, regardless of their guilt or innocence.

It is a singularly successful tool in the effort to divide and conquer the working classes of America, historically used by both of our political parties to wage war against each other and the working classes.

They protect those in power, even as they sow seeds of discourse through the masses: seeds of fear, division, hatred, and dishonesty. We are soon so blinded by hatred for our neighbors that we are unable to see the chains fastened to our legs, chains we all share. These are the facts. The "looming threat" of cultural Marxism is simply the most recent manifestation of this grand illusion.

There is no proof of a genuine cultural Marxist movement in the U.S. Using political correctness to bring about socialism or communism is a direct contradiction of their philosophical understanding. The boogeyman they're trying to sell you is not based on any tangible, shared reality. It is simply a means of engendering alarmism, using a theory rooted in antisemitism, spread by those who refuse to even try to understand other cultures or changes within their own culture.

We cannot cling to ignorance if we hope to find that truth, if we hope it to ever evolve beyond our maddening cycles of predictable self-destruction, we must not allow our misguided perspectives to drive us to action.

For inspiration, I will leave you with one final thought from Marcus Aurelius, an Emperor who ruled Rome in the first century AD. This quote hangs in my office at the time of this writing and is one to which I have often turned in times of doubt or trepidation.

"The first rule is to keep an untroubled spirit. The second is to look things in the face and know them for what they are." (Aurelius, n.d.)

References

Academic Dictionaries and Encyclopedias. (n.d.). *Pentagram*. Retrieved July 12, 2021, from https://en-academic.com/dic.nsf/enwiki/130099#European_occultism

Activities, Committee on Un-American. (2019). *Investigation of un-american propaganda activities in the United States: Hearings before a special committee on un-American activities, house of . . . 23, 24, 31, and June 1, 1939 at Washington*. Forgotten Books.

Adhamy, A. (2021, June 24). *Why did Hitler choose the swastika, and how did a Sanskrit symbol become a Nazi emblem?* HistoryExtra. https://www.historyextra.com/period/second-world-war/how-why-sanskrit-symbol-become-nazi-swastika-svastika/

Alberta, T. (n.d.). *Nikki Haley's time for choosing*. Politico. Retrieved July 12, 2021, from https://www.politico.com/interactives/2021/magazine-nikki-haleys-choice/

Allebach, N. (2020, December 7). *The difference between real conspiracies and conspiracy theories*. Medium. https://nathanallebach.medium.com/the-difference-between-real-conspiracies-and-conspiracy-theories-9c14d369cafe

American rhetoric: Ronald Reagan -- Radio address on socialized medicine. (201–08-03). American Rhetoric Online Speech Bank. https://www.americanrhetoric.com/speeches/ronaldreagansocializedmedicine.htm

Appleton Public Library Wisconsin. (n.d.). *Joseph McCarthy: Biography*. Appleton Public Library. Retrieved July 12, 2021, from https://apl.org/community/mccarthy

Aurelius, M. (n.d.). A quote from Meditations. Goodreads. Retrieved July 20, 2021, from https://www.goodreads.com/quotes/20870-the-first-rule-is-to-keep-an-untroubled-spirit-the

Avrich, P. (1996). *Sacco and Vanzetti: The anarchist background*. Princeton University Press.

Bartlett, B. (2020, August 17). *Socialism is as American as apple pie*. The New Republic. https://newrepublic.com/article/158921/socialism-american-pence-biden-sanders-2020-election

Baum, G., & Miller, D. (2012, November 19). *The Hollywood Reporter, after 65 years, addresses role in blacklist*. Hollywood Reporter. https://www.hollywoodreporter.com/tv/tv-features/blacklist-thr-addresses-role-65-391931/

Beichman, A. (2006, February 1). *The politics of personal self-destruction*. Hoover Institution. https://www.hoover.org/research/politics-personal-self-destruction

BLACKPAST. (2019, August 8). (1857) *Frederick Douglass, "If there is no struggle, there is no progress."* https://www.blackpast.org/african-american-history/1857-frederick-douglass-if-there-no-struggle-there-no-progress/

Boyd, C. L. (n.d.). *Sedition act of 1918*. The First Amendment Encyclopedia. Retrieved July 12, 2021, from https://www.mtsu.edu/first-amendment/article/1239/sedition-act-of-1918

Bytwerk, R. (n.d.). *Goebbels on communism with the mask off*. Calvin University German Propaganda Archives. Retrieved July 17, 2021, from https://research.calvin.edu/german-propaganda-archive/goeb58.htm

Brianton, K. (2019, June 28). *Waldorf Declaration*. Cinema History Online. https://cinemahistoryonline.com/tag/waldorf-declaration/

Campbell, O. (2018, May 30). *Here's what happened when Reagan went after healthcare programs. It's not good*. Medium. https://timeline.com/reagan-trump-healthcare-cuts-8cf64aa242eb

Campion, M. J. (2014, October 23). *How the world loved the swastika - until Hitler stole it*. BBC News. https://www.bbc.com/news/magazine-29644591

Center for Political Education. (2017). *Marxism 101 timeline*. https://politicaleducation.org/wp-content/uploads/2017/09/Marx-Timeline-Exercise.Marxism-101.2017.pdf

Corradetti, C. (n.d.). *Frankfurt School and critical theory*. Internet Encyclopedia of Philosophy. Retrieved July 12, 2021, from https://iep.utm.edu/frankfur/

Cox, R. (2020, August 28). *Republicans mostly rant about fake socialism*. Reuters. https://www.reuters.com/article/us-usa-election-convention-breakingviews/breakingviews-cox-republicans-mostly-rant-about-fake-socialism-idUSKBN25O1QT

Crowder, O. (n.d.). *Seattle general strike*. University of Washington Civil Rights and Labor History Consortium. Retrieved July 12, 2021, from http://depts.washington.edu/labhist/strike/

Cunningham, R. K. (2017, January 25). *Orwell, Nineteen Eighty-Four, and political words*. Illinois Press Blog. https://www.press.uillinois.edu/wordpress/orwell-nineteen-eighty-four-and-political-words/

Douglas, W. O. (1952, January 13). *The black silence of fear*. The New York Times. https://www.nytimes.com/1952/01/13/archives/the-black-silence-of-fear-if-we-are-afraid-of-ideas-justice-douglas.html

Douglass, F. (1886). *Americans who tell the truth*. https://www.americanswhotellthetruth.org/portraits/frederick-douglass

Encyclopedia of Anti-Revisionism On-Line. (n.d.). *The struggle for black liberation and socialist revolution*. Marxists.Org. Retrieved July 12, 2021, from https://www.marxists.org/history/erol/ncm-3/ol-black-liberation-3/chapter1.htm

ENGELSTAD, E., & KRISTJÁNSSON, M. (2019, February 6). *The return of "Judeo-Bolshevism."* Jacobin. https://www.jacobinmag.com/2019/02/antisemitism-judaism-bolsheviks-socialists-conspiracy-theories

Federal Bureau of Investigation. (2020, March 18). *Alger Hiss*. https://www.fbi.gov/history/famous-cases/alger-hiss

Fernholz, E. M. (n.d.). *The Russian Revolution of 1917*. Marquette University History Department. Retrieved July 12, 2021, from https://academic.mu.edu/meissnerd/russian-rev.htm

Foner, P. S. (1986). *May Day: A short history of the International Workers' Holiday, 1886–1986* (1st ed.). International Publishers.

Ford, A. (2012, March 6). *Charles Dickens: the making of a great writer*. Socialism Today. http://socialismtoday.org/archive/156/dickens.html

Gavrilets, S., & Vose, A. (2006). The dynamics of Machiavellian intelligence. *Proceedings of the National Academy of Sciences, 103*(45), 16823–16828. https://doi.org/10.1073/pnas.0601428103

Goodman, W. (1969). *The Committee: The Extraordinary Career of the House Committee on Un-American Activities* (1st ed.). Penguin Books; Pelican.

Gordon, B. (2001). *Hollywood Exile, or How I Learned to Love the Blacklist (Texas Film and Media Studies Series)*. University of Texas Press.

Grey, J. (2020, May 6). *How Machiavelli was misunderstood*. Newstatesman. https://www.newstatesman.com/machiavelli-his-life-and-times-alexander-lee-review

Hanebrink, P. (2020). *A Specter Haunting Europe: The Myth of Judeo-Bolshevism*. Belknap Press: An Imprint of Harvard University Press.

Hanson, O. (2017). *Americanism versus Bolshevism (Classic Reprint)*. Fb&c Limited.

Harris, C. (2016, December 27). *The murder of Rasputin, 100 Years Later*. Smithsonian Magazine. https://www.smithsonianmag.com/history/murder-rasputin-100-years-later-180961572/

Hess, J. Z. (2021, June 11). *What does a Marxist think of Bernie? Q&A with Arthur Peña*. Public Square Magazine. https://publicsquaremag.org/politics-law/what-does-a-marxist-think-of-bernie-qa-with-arthur-pena/

Hill, M. (2017, September 28). *A Marxist exploration: Bernie Sanders, political revolution, and socialism*. Freedom Socialist Party. https://socialism.com/fs-article/a-marxist-exploration-bernie-sanders-political-revolution-and-socialism/

History.com Editors. (2019, December 4). *Cold War history*. HISTORY. https://www.history.com/topics/cold-war/cold-war-history

Hockett, R. (2020, February 20). *Choose your "socialism."* Forbes. https://www.forbes.com/sites/rhockett/2020/02/20/choose-your-socialism/

House Un-American Activities Committee. (2003). The Eleanor Roosevelt Papers. https://web.archive.org/web/20100529011543/http://www.nps.gov/archive/elro/glossary/huac.htm

Hristov, T. (2020). *Impossible knowledge: Conspiracy theories, power, and truth* (1st ed.). Routledge.

Industrial Workers of the World. (1905). Preamble to the IWW Constitution. IWW Archive. https://archive.iww.org/culture/official/preamble/

Institute for Public Affairs. (2020, September 5). *The Republican Party's puzzling obsession with socialism*. In These Times. https://inthesetimes.com/article/rnc-socialism-republican-convention-trump-2020

Internet Encyclopedia of Philosophy. (n.d.). *Fallacies |*. Retrieved July 12, 2021, from https://iep.utm.edu/fallacy/

J. (2019, August 7). *The history and symbolism of the pentagram*. Dualcrossroads. https://www.dualcrossroads.com/post/the-history-and-symbolism-of-the-pentagram

Johansson, M. (n.d.). *Sweden's welfare state; myths and realities: a Marxist analysis of the 'Nordic Model.'* Marxists.Org. Retrieved July 12, 2021, from https://www.marxists.org/history/etol/newspape/irishmr/vol01/no03/johansson.pdf

Jones, J. (2016, September 2). *The red menace: A striking gallery of anti-communist posters, ads, comic books, magazines & films*. Open Culture. https://www.openculture.com/2014/11/the-red-menace-a-striking-gallery-of-anti-communist-propaganda.html

Jones, S. (2020, August 25). *The GOP thinks Marxists are taking over. If only that were true*. Intelligencer. https://nymag.com/intelligencer/2020/08/the-gops-red-baiting-is-a-lie-of-omission.html

Kampf Lassin, M. (n.d.). *Trump is running scared of socialism*. Jacobin. Retrieved July 12, 2021, from https://jacobinmag.com/2018/10/socialism-report-white-house-trump-medicare-for-all

Kellner, D. (n.d.). *Cultural Marxism and cultural studies.* UCLA School of Education and Information Studies. Retrieved July 12, 2021, from https://pages.gseis.ucla.edu/faculty/kellner/essays/culturalmarxism.pdf

Keshavarzi, A. (2012). Charles Dickens: a reformist or a compromiser. *Rupkatha Journal on Interdisciplinary Studies in Humanities, 4*(1). http://rupkatha.com/V4/n1/14_Charles_Dickens_a_Reformer.pdf

Klippenstein, K. (2021, March 3). *Trump administration referred a record number of leaks for criminal investigation.* The Intercept. https://theintercept.com/2021/03/02/trump-leaks-criminal-investigation/

Knight, B. (2021, April 8). *Socialism is an idea, not the Boogeyman.* The McDonough County Voice. https://eu.mcdonoughvoice.com/story/opinion/columns/2021/04/08/socialism-idea-not-boogeyman/7145553002/

Krausz, T. (2019, June 13). *Of Jews, Bolsheviks and blood libel.* The Jerusalem Post. https://www.jpost.com/diaspora/of-jews-and-bolsheviks-592445

Kruse, M. (2015, July 17). *14 things Bernie Sanders has said about socialism.* POLITICO. https://www.politico.com/story/2015/07/14-things-bernie-sanders-has-said-about-socialism-120265

Labor Movement. (2015, July 15). *Visual propaganda: Ideology in art.* https://ideologicalart.com/labor-movement/

Lang, J. M. (2016, January 12). *What Republicans can learn from George Orwell — It's not what you think.* WBUR.Org. https://www.wbur.org/cognoscenti/2016/01/12/1984-donald-trump-rand-paul-ted-cruz-james-m-lang

Letourneau, J. (2008). Xenophobia in the 1920s. *DuPage Anthology of Academic Writing Across the Curriculum, 6*(30). https://dc.cod.edu/cgi/viewcontent.cgi?article=1072&context=essai

Levit, K. R., Olin, G. L., & Letch, S. W. (1992). Americans' health insurance coverage, 1980–91. *Health Care Financing Review, 14*(1), 31–57. https://www.ncbi.nlm.nih.gov/pmc/articles/PMC4193314/

Litke, E. (2020, March 4). *PolitiFact - No, Bernie Sanders is not a communist, contrary to Scott Walker claim.* Politifact. https://www.politifact.com/factchecks/2020/mar/04/scott-walker/no-bernie-sanders-not-communist/

Lynn, A. (2018). Cultural Marxism. *The hedgehog review, 20*(3). https://hedgehogreview.com/issues/the-evening-of-life/articles/cultural-marxism

Machiavelli: A man misunderstood. (2005, March 12). The Age. https://www.theage.com.au/entertainment/books/machiavelli-a-man-misunderstood-20050312-gdzrjv.html

Machiavelli, N., & Marriott, W. K. (2017). *The Prince* (1st ed.). CreateSpace Independent Publishing Platform.

MacLeod, A. (2019, February 8). *'Venezuela': Media's one-word rebuttal to the threat of socialism*. FAIR. https://fair.org/home/venezuela-medias-one-word-rebuttal-to-the-threat-of-socialism/

Martelle, C. (2004). *Fanning the flames: Interpretations and reactions to McCarthyism*. EDUCATION AND HUMAN DEVELOPMENT MASTER'S THESES. https://digitalcommons.brockport.edu/ehd_theses/592/

Mayer, M. (2021). *They thought they were free: The Germans, 1933–45* (Unabridged ed.). Tantor and Blackstone Publishing.

McCarthyism [ushistory.org]. (n.d.). Ushistory.Org. Retrieved July 12, 2021, from https://www.ushistory.org/us/53a.asp

McDermott, M. (2021, April 26). *10 things you need to know about the swastika*. Hindu American Foundation. https://www.hinduamerican.org/blog/10-things-you-need-to-know-about-the-swastika/

McKay, A. (2020, August 3). *Scandinavian 'socialism': The truth of the Nordic model*. Life in Norway. https://www.lifeinnorway.net/scandinavian-socialism/

McLellan, D. (2006). *Karl Marx: A Biography; Fourth Edition* (4th ed.). Palgrave Macmillan.

McNamera, R. (2019, June 23). *Committee on Public Information, America's WWI propaganda Agency*. ThoughtCo. https://www.thoughtco.com/committee-on-public-information-4691743

Monahan, S. (n.d.). *Reading Paine from the left*. Jacobin. Retrieved July 12, 2021, from https://www.jacobinmag.com/2015/03/thomas-paine-american-revolution-common-sense/

Morning Edition. (2007, December 6). *Socialized medicine belittled on campaign trail*. National Public Radio. https://www.npr.org/templates/story/story.php?storyId=16962482

Murray, R. K. (1980). *Red scare study in national hysteria: 1919–1920*. Greenwood Pub Group.

Myre, G. (2017, June 28). *Once reserved for spies, espionage act now used against suspected leakers*. National Public Radio. https://choice.npr.org/index.html?origin=https://www.npr.org/sections/paralle

ls/2017/06/28/534682231/once-reserved-for-spies-espionage-act-now-used-against-suspected-leakers

NCC Staff. (2021, January 2). *On this day, massive raids during the red scare.* National Constitution Center – Constitutioncenter.Org. https://constitutioncenter.org/blog/on-this-day-massive-raids-during-the-red-scare

Nederman, C. (2019, May 28). *Niccolò Machiavelli.* The Stanford Encyclopedia of Philosophy. https://plato.stanford.edu/entries/machiavelli/

Newton, M. (2020). *The Ku Klux Klan in Mississippi: A history* (Reprint ed.). McFarland.

Norberg, J. (2020). *Sweden's lessons for America.* Cato Institute. https://www.cato.org/policy-report/january/february-2020/swedens-lessons-america

Parfitt, S. (2016). *The justice department campaign against the IWW, 1917–1920.* University of Washington. https://depts.washington.edu/iww/justice_dept.shtml

Perry, D. M. (2019, July 12). *What's so scary about socialism? - GEN.* Medium. https://gen.medium.com/whats-so-scary-about-socialism-4ae6d336620e

Pike, W. E. (2006, December 1). *Was Dickens really a socialist?* Foundation for Economic Education. https://fee.org/articles/was-dickens-really-a-socialist/

Public Broadcasting Service. (n.d.). *Frederick Douglass.* PBS. Retrieved July 12, 2021, from https://www.pbs.org/wgbh/aia/part4/4p1539.html

Roy, A. (2018, May 25). *Why Ronald Reagan embraced universal coverage.* Medium. https://freopp.org/why-ronald-reagan-embraced-universal-coverage-1a024e3e74b3

Schmidt, R. (2000). *Red scare: FBI and the origins of anticommunism in the United States, 1919–1943* (1st ed.). Museum Tusculanum Press.

Schrecker, E. W., & Deery, P. (2016). *The age of McCarthyism: A brief history with documents (Bedford cultural editions)* (Third ed.). Bedford/St. Martin's.

Schwartz, J. (2019, July 1). *How socialism made America great.* The Daily Beast. https://www.thedailybeast.com/how-socialism-made-america-great

Schwartz, R. A. (1999). *How the film and television blacklists worked.* Florida International University. https://comptalk.fiu.edu/blacklist.htm

Shakespeare, W. (n.d.). *Othello.* Massachusetts Institute of Technology. Retrieved July 20, 2021, from http://shakespeare.mit.edu/othello/full.html

Sheridan, F., & Leslie, L. (1997). *A user's guide to the federal theater project. OAH Magazine of History, 11*(2), 50–52. https://doi.org/10.1093/maghis/11.2.50

Sherman, A. (2020, October 15). *PolitiFact - Trump's false claim that Biden is a socialist*. Politifact. https://www.politifact.com/factchecks/2020/oct/15/donald-trump/trumps-false-claim-biden-socialist/

Silverman, A. G. (2021, April 20). *We're not socialists. Let's say so. | Opinion | The Harvard Crimson*. The Harvard Crimson. https://www.thecrimson.com/column/granola-advocacy/article/2021/4/20/silverman-were-not-socialists-lets-say-so/

Sion, B. (2009, May 12). *Conspiracy theories and the jews*. My Jewish Learning. https://www.myjewishlearning.com/article/conspiracy-theories-the-jews/

Social Security Administration. (n.d.). *Social security history*. Retrieved July 12, 2021, from https://www.ssa.gov/history/tally65.html

Society of Independent Motion Picture Producers. (2005). *The SIMPP president explains the Hollywood blacklist to its members*. Hollywood Renegades Archive. http://cobbles.com/simpp_archive/huac_nelson1947.htm

Spielberger, D. (2018, October 25). *What the right gets wrong about Venezuela and the American left*. Think Progress. https://archive.thinkprogress.org/right-obsession-venezuela-socialism-completely-disregards-history-861a959eb8f3/

Stanley, B. (2021, March 14). *Twenty years before sweeping health funding cuts, an anti-medicare vinyl gave President Reagan his political start*. The Rotation. https://the-rotation.com/a-record-from-ronnie-how-an-anti-medicare-vinyl-gave-a-future-president-his-political-start-and-changed-american-health-care-forever/

Storrs, L. R. Y. (2015, July 2). *McCarthyism and the second red scare*. Oxford Research Encyclopedia of American History. https://americanhistory.oxfordre.com/view/10.1093/acrefore/9780199329175.001.0001/acrefore-9780199329175-e-6

Strata: Pentagrams in Judea. (2017, February 9). The BAS Library. https://www.baslibrary.org/biblical-archaeology-review/39/6/18

The British Library. (n.d.). *Machiavelli's The Prince*. Retrieved July 12, 2021, from https://www.bl.uk/collection-items/machiavellis-the-prince#

The Council of Economic Advisors. (2018, August). *The opportunity costs of socialism*. https://trumpwhitehouse.archives.gov/wp-content/uploads/2018/10/The-Opportunity-Costs-of-Socialism.pdf

The Editors of Encyclopaedia Britannica. (2021, April 27). *Haymarket affair | History, aftermath, & influence*. Encyclopedia Britannica. https://www.britannica.com/event/Haymarket-Affair

Tindera, M. (2020, September 21). *Biden pulls away in race for billionaire donors, with 131 to Trump's 99.* Forbes. https://www.forbes.com/sites/michelatindera/2020/08/08/biden-pulls-away-in-race-for-billionaire-donors/?sh=438080543b62

Transparency International. (2020). *Corruption perceptions index 2020.* https://www.transparency.org/en/cpi/2020/index/nzl#

Truman, H. S. (1952, October 10). President Truman, Rear Platform Remarks, Syracuse, New York. Truman Library. https://www.trumanlibrary.gov/soundrecording-records/sr59-160-president-truman-rear-platform-remarks-syracuse-new-york

United States, United States, & United States. Congress. House. Committee on Education and Labor. (1947). *Index to legislative reorganization act of 1946 (public law 601, 79th congress, appended).* U.S. Government Printing Office.

von Mises, L. (2017, December 22). *Marxism unmasked: From delusion to destruction.* Foundation for Economic Education. https://fee.org/resources/marxism-unmasked-from-delusion-to-destruction/?gclid=CjoKCQjw8vqGBhC_ARIsADMSd1CcsRoh2aNzhogj6LrVh7hy2AQLutjWFxMN8eaHBMWj52Fq_j3BFkoaAtk-EALw_wcB

Whitcomb, N. A. (2021, February 2). *Nordic social democracy in US politics.* Aarhus University. https://nordics.info/themes/nordic-social-democracy-in-us-politics/

Why George Orwell's 1984 still matters, 70 years since publication. (2019, September 6). Canadian Broadcasting Corporation. https://www.cbc.ca/radio/writersandcompany/why-george-orwell-s-1984-still-matters-70-years-since-publication-1.5272470

Wikipedia contributors. (2021, February 19). *Machiavellianism.* Wikipedia. https://en.wikipedia.org/wiki/Machiavellianism

Wolfe, L. R. (2019, January 22). *The first red scare: A timeline.* Cold War Studies. https://coldwarstudies.com/2013/04/24/the-first-red-scare-a-timeline/

阳鱼太. (2020, December 11). *Adam Smith's socialism.* Medium. https://taiyangyu.medium.com/adam-smiths-socialism-83259d81a3ee

www.ingramcontent.com/pod-product-compliance
Lightning Source LLC
Chambersburg PA
CBHW061512250726
48657CB00005B/1815